# Practically RAW

## Desserts

# Also by Amber Shea Crawley

**Practically Raw:** Flexible Raw Recipes Anyone Can Make

# Practically RAW
## Desserts

## Flexible Recipes for All-Natural Sweets and Treats

Amber Shea Crawley

**VEGAN HERITAGE PRESS**

Woodstock • Virginia

***Practically Raw Desserts: Flexible Recipes for All-Natural Sweets and Treats*** by
Amber Shea Crawley (Copyright © 2013 by Amber Shea Crawley)

Printed in the United States of America
10  9  8  7  6  5  4  3  2 1

ISBN 13: 978-0-9800131-8-4
ISBN 10: 0-9800131-8-6

First Edition

Vegan Heritage Press books are available at quantity discounts. For information, please visit our website at www.veganheritagepress.com or write the publisher at Vegan Heritage Press, P.O. Box 628, Woodstock, VA 22664-0628.

Library of Congress Cataloging-in-Publication Data

Crawley, Amber Shea, 1985-
 Practically raw desserts : flexible raw recipes for all-natural sweets and treats / by Amber Shea Crawley. -- First edition.
    pages cm
 Includes bibliographical references and index.
 ISBN 978-0-9800131-8-4 (pbk.)
 1.  Desserts. 2.  Raw foods.  I. Title.
 TX773.C676 2013
 641.86--dc23
                                2012045883

Photos: Cover photos by the author (clockwise from top left): German Chocolate Cake, page 92; Tropical Fruit Tartlets, page 133; Strawberries & Crème Tart, page 138; Tuxedo Cheesecake Brownies, page 70; Ice Creams, pages 156-157; author photo by Russell James. Interior recipe photos by the author. Photos of the author on pages viii and 204 by Stephen Melvin. Spot illustrations of individual ingredients from stock photo sources.

**Disclaimer:** The information provided in this book should not be taken as medical advice. If you require a medical diagnosis or prescription, or if you are contemplating any major dietary change, please consult a qualified health-care provider. You should always seek an expert medical opinion before making changes in your diet or supplementation regimen.

**Publisher's Note:** The information in this book is correct and complete to the best of our knowledge. Website addresses and contact information were correct at the time of publication. The publisher is not responsible for specific health or allergy issues or adverse reactions to recipes contained in this book.

## Dedication

To all my blog readers and online friends of chefambershea.com:
Your years of support and readership mean the world to me!

# Contents

Dedication     v

## 1. How Sweet It Is     1
*Flexibility, Ingredients, Tips, Tricks*

Why Raw Desserts?     2
Ingredient Guide     4
Equipment Guide     16
Pantry List     18
Tips and Tricks     20
Options Guide     21

## 2. Back to Basics     23
*Milks, Butters, Flours, Syrups*

Nondairy Milks     25
  Nut Milk     25
  Instant Nut Milk     26
  Seed Milk     27
  Instant Seed Milk     27
  Coconut Milk     28
  Oat Milk     28
Flours     29
  Almond Flour     29
  Instant Almond Flour     30
  Cashew Flour     30
  Sunflour     31
  Oat Flour     32
Butters     33
  Almond Butter     33
  Cashew Butter     35
  Coconut Butter     36
  Sunseed Butter     37
Other     38
  Date Syrup     38
  Instant Applesauce     39

## 3. One Smart Cookie     41
*Cookies, Biscuits, Macaroons*

Chocolate Chunk Cookies     42
Sugar Cookie Cutouts     44
Midnight Mocha Cookies     46
Russian Tea Cakes     49
Chewy Oatmeal Raisin Cookies     50
Cherry Almond Cookies     52
Nutty Buddy Sandwiches     54
Chocolate Walnut Drop Cookies     57
Jam Thumbprint Cookies     58
Pecan Shortbread Cookies     60
Detox Macaroons     62
Protein Crinkle Cookies     63

## 4. A Girl Walks into a Bar...     65
*Bars, Brownies, Blondies*

Ultimate Raw Brownies     67
Banana Butter Brownies     68
Tuxedo Cheesecake Brownies     70
Famous Five-Minute Blondies II     73
Strawberry Blondies     74
White Chocolate Macadamia Nut
  Blondies     76
Baklava Blondies     79
Goji Berry Granola Bars     80
Marzipan Buckeye Bars     82
Cherry-Carob Bars     84
Pecan Chai Spice Bars     85
Matt's Banana-Oat Breakfast Bars     86

## 5. A Piece of Cake     89
*Cakes, Cupcakes, Cheesecakes, Tortes*

Confetti Birthday Cake     90
German Chocolate Cake     92
Enlightened Carrot Cake     94
Maple Streusel Coffee Cake
  Squares     97

Pineapple Upside-Down Cake 98
Austrian Sacher Torte 100
Crumb-Topped Chocolate
    Hazelnut Torte 102
New York Cheesecake 104
Lemon Love Cupcakes 106
Devil's Food Cupcakes 109
Strawberry Shortcupcakes 110
Coconut Heaven Cupcakes 113
Almond Butter Banana Cupcakes 114

## 6. Square Root of Pie 117
*Pies, Tarts, Cobblers, Crisps*

Deep-Dish Caramel Apple Pie 118
Key Lime Pie 121
French Silk Pie 122
Blueberry Dream Pie 124
Coco-Nana Cream Pie 127
Summer Fruit Pizza 128
Dark Chocolate Truffle Tart with
    Macaroon Crust 130
Tropical Fruit Tartlets 133
Linzer Torte 134
Individual Cherry Crumbles 137
Strawberries & Crème Tart 138
Vanilla Bean Peach Cobbler 140

## 7. The Proof Is in the Pudding 143
*Ice Creams, Puddings, Mousses*

Easy Chia Pudding 144
Velvety Chocolate Mousse 147
Not-Your-Grandma's Banana
    Pudding 148
Protein Power Pudding 150
Dulce de Leche Spooncream 151
Kheer (Indian Rice Pudding) 152
Sugar-Free Chocolate Pudding 154
Create-Your-Own Ice Cream 156
Mango-Pistachio Kulfi Pops 159
Dark Chocolate Sorbet 160

Banana Soft-Serve 162
Gelato di Avocado 163

## 8. Adventures in Candyland 165
*Chocolates, Candies, Fudge, Truffles*

Easy Chocolate Bar 166
Salted Tahini Caramels 169
Coconut Butter Fudge 170
Cocoa Crunch Clusters 171
Classic Cacao Truffles 172
White Chocolate Vanilla Bean
    Truffles 174
Lemon Poppyseed Truffles 175
Jingle Balls 176
Turtle Bites 177
Almond Butter Melties 178
Superfood Snackers 180
Cashew Butter Cups 182
Chocolate Protein Bark 184

## 9. To Top It All Off 187
*Frostings, Glazes, Drizzles, Ganaches*

Vanilla-Coconut Crème 188
Fluffy Chocolate Frosting 189
Tangy Cream Cheese Icing 190
Ooey Gooey Caramel Sauce 191
Raspberry Coulis 192
Coconut Lemon Curd 193
Sugar-Free Chocolate Ganache 194
Fat-Free Chocolate Syrup 195
Fruity Chia Jam 196

## 10. Resources 199
*Ingredients, Equipment, Education*

Acknowledgments 205
About the Author 206
Index 207

# How Sweet It Is

## Flexibility, Ingredients, Tips, Tricks

*E*veryone seems to be seeking healthier alternatives to traditional snacks and sweets, whether it means foods low in added sugars, comprised of whole, natural, unprocessed ingredients, or free of animal-based products. In addition, interest in raw food is growing at a fevered pace, as are the gluten- and allergen-free markets, soy- and oil-free dieting, attention to the glycemic index of food and sweets, and even grain-free/"paleolithic" styles of eating. It is rare for all these audiences to be satisfied by a single food, but it is rarer still – in fact, thus far, it is unheard of – to find all these considerations addressed in an entire collection of dessert recipes – until now!

*Practically Raw Desserts: Flexible Recipes for All-Natural Sweets and Treats* is a treasure trove of delectable raw cakes, cookies, bars, brownies, pies, puddings, candies, pastries, and even frozen treats. All of the recipes in this book can be made 100% raw or adapted to a non-raw kitchen. For every recipe, I provide numerous ingredient substitution possibilities as well as the option to bake, instead of dehydrate, any of my treats that require it.

Besides being refreshingly flexible, every recipe in this book has the added bonus of being free of dairy, eggs, gluten, wheat, soy, peanuts, corn, refined grains, refined sugars, yeast, starch, and other nutrient-poor ingredients. Many recipes are free of grains, oils, nuts, and added sugars as well, and when they're not, I often provide variations to make them so. As in my first book, *Practically Raw,* a nutritional breakdown is included with every recipe.

Most importantly, these desserts are mouthwateringly scrumptious. Inside *Practically Raw Desserts,* you'll find everything from family favorites like Sugar Cookie Cutouts and Key Lime Pie to innovative or exotic delicacies like Austrian Sacher Torte and Baklava Blondies. The result is a collection of tantalizing *and* accessible sweets and treats that are sure to impress and delight.

Whether you're trying to eliminate allergens, watch your sugar or grain intake, or simply feed your family cleaner treats; whether you subscribe to a diet based on whole, natural foods; or whether you're avoiding animal products – or any, all, or even none of the above – my practically raw desserts have plenty of sweet rewards to offer you.

## Why Raw Desserts?

Everyone deserves to have some sweet treats in their diet. I, for one, couldn't do without them. If we're going to indulge our taste buds in a decadent dessert, why not reap some nutritional and lifestyle benefits at the same time?

### For Your Health

**Nutrient dense:** Raw desserts are packed with healthy, unprocessed ingredients that contain their full spectrum of undisturbed vitamins, minerals, and other nutrients. Water-soluble vitamins (including vitamin C and all B-complex vitamins) and antioxidants, which are susceptible to heat damage and are often lost through the processes of cooking and baking, are abundant in raw treats.

**Healthy fats:** Certain fats, especially delicate unsaturated fats (including essential fatty acids like omega-3s and -6s), are extremely sensitive to heat and can turn into trans fats when cooked. As often as possible, you should eat your fats in their raw forms to avoid the carcinogenic potential of heated fats and oils that can so easily turn rancid. Raw desserts, naturally, contain only healthy raw fats!

**Enzymes:** Also killed by heat, the food enzymes present in raw desserts can potentially aid our own digestive enzymes in breaking down and absorbing nutrients in the stomach.

**Fiber and protein:** My treats are significantly higher in both fiber and protein than conventional baked goods.

**Allergen-free:** Raw desserts are naturally free of most common allergens, such as gluten, wheat, soy, eggs, milk, and peanuts. The notable exception to this is tree nuts, which are common in raw food, but I made sure to include plenty of nut-free recipes and variations in this book as well! You can enjoy raw desserts without worrying about the majority of common food allergies and intolerances and the gastrointestinal distress they can cause.

**Elimination of processed foods:** White flours, refined sugars, and other over-processed ingredients are nowhere to be found in wholesome raw desserts.

## For Your Lifestyle

**Practical:** The vast majority of these recipes don't need to be dehydrated or baked at all, and when they do, I provide directions on how to make them in a dehydrator *or* an oven (and sometimes even a third option to freeze or serve as-is!). I'm not fussy about making sure everything is "truly raw"—you'll see I like to use non-raw ingredients such as maple syrup and plain old-fashioned rolled oats sometimes. My substitution lists will often give you non-raw options to swap in for raw ingredients.

**Flexible:** Speaking of substitution lists, I provide one with every recipe. If you don't have ingredient "x," don't hesitate to sub in ingredient "y" from the list below the recipe. I strive to make my recipes doable by anyone and everyone, no matter what your budget (or pantry) looks like.

**Speedy to make:** Raw desserts are the ultimate in instant gratification. Almost all the recipes in this book can be put together in 30 minutes or less, without ever having to turn on an oven!

**Low-maintenance:** Baked goods can be finicky—you often have to treat batters and doughs delicately and take care not to overmix or overbake things. Raw treats are far more forgiving.

**Customizable:** You can *always* feel free to flex your pastry chef muscles with my recipes. Try any of my ideas for tweaks and variations, or invent your own. Be creative and have fun with it.

**Kid-friendly:**  Children will love these desserts, and can often even help you in the process of making them. My treats are a great way to teach healthy indulgence.

**Animal-free:** Since raw desserts contain no eggs or dairy, they are suitable for vegans and strict vegetarians. I have even declined to include honey in my recipes in order to keep them 100% vegan (though you may substitute at your discretion).

Though it sounds almost too good to be true, when it comes to raw food, eating dessert is actually good for you!

## Something for Every Body

No matter what your dietary needs are, I've got you covered in this collection of decadent – yet healthful – pastries and sweets.

*All* of the recipes in this book are raw, vegan, low-glycemic, and free of dairy, eggs, gluten, wheat, soy, refined sugars, refined flours, yeast, starches, gums, corn, and peanuts. Moreover, they all contain fewer than 300 calories (and often considerably less) per serving!

*Many* of the recipes are also free of grains, oils, nuts, and added sugars.

*All* of the recipes provide nutritional information, numerous ingredient substitution options, baking directions for using a conventional oven (if applicable), and fun and creative variations to stretch your desserts repertoire even further.

*Many* of the recipes also provide lower-fat, lower-sugar, nut-free, grain-free, and/or oil-free variations when possible, and chef's tips to help streamline or enhance the recipe.

In other words, these recipes are perfect for:

- Raw foodists and raw food dabblers
- Vegetarians and vegans
- Those with celiac disease or gluten sensitivity
- Those with allergies or intolerances to dairy, eggs, soy, corn, and more
- Low-glycemic (low-sugar) dieters
- Paleo/Primal (grain-free, refined-sugar-free) dieters
- Oil-free/whole-foods dieters
- Calorie counters and the health-conscious
- Seasoned bakers wishing to try their hand at something new
- Kitchen klutzes or oven-phobes who feel they can't bake at all
- Parents wanting to feed their children wholesome treats
- Children themselves
- *Anyone* with a sweet tooth!

## Ingredient Guide

Roll up your sleeves and get ready for a crash course on all the goodies that go into making gourmet raw sweets. Here's everything you need to know about the tasty and healthful ingredients that will play a part in the desserts you'll soon be crafting.

If you have questions on where to purchase any of the ingredients or brands mentioned here, visit the Resources section beginning on page 199.

### Nuts

Nuts are a jack-of-all-trades in raw desserts. They can be chopped, crushed, blended, or used whole. They can add texture, flavor, crunch, or creaminess to a dish. They can even be turned into milks and flours. Whenever possible, buy organic raw nuts rather than roasted and/or salted varieties; however, in a pinch, you can use roasted, unsalted varieties. All nuts contain good amounts of healthy fats (particularly monounsaturated fat), fiber, protein, and minerals. Many nuts are also a great source of fat-soluble vitamins, particularly vitamin E. Store raw nuts in your fridge or freezer so their delicate oils don't go rancid.

- **Almonds:** Probably the most all-purpose nut in the raw food world, almonds make beautiful milks (pages 24-25), flours (pages 29-30), and nut butters (pages 33-34), and they're rich in calcium and vitamin E to boot. All almonds labeled "raw" in the

United States are actually pasteurized. Truly-raw almonds can be ordered online, either imported from Italy or direct from American farmers, but plain-old store-bought "raw" almonds will work perfectly fine in my recipes.

- **Brazil nuts:** The world's best source of the trace mineral selenium, which is important for proper thyroid function, just one Brazil nut supplies 100% of the RDA.

- **Cashews:** Since they must be steamed to be removed from their shells, cashews aren't truly raw. Nonetheless, thanks to their beautiful creaminess and slight sweetness, they're an important component of many raw desserts. They're also a good source of magnesium, which is vital for healthy muscles and bones.

- **Hazelnuts:** Also called "filberts," hazelnuts contain a great deal of folate, an important B vitamin that helps build and repair DNA. They're super-crunchy and go great with chocolate.

- **Macadamia nuts:** Macadamias contain more healthful monounsaturated fats and fewer pro-inflammatory omega-6 fats than any other nut. Rich, buttery-tasting macadamias can be used for creaminess in the same way cashews can.

- **Pecans:** Pecans are one of my favorite nuts in the world for their toasty flavor and rich texture. They also contain more antioxidants than any other nut.

- **Pistachios:** The lowest-calorie nut, pistachios possess an unmistakable (and lovely) green hue and an addictive crunch.

- **Walnuts:** More anti-inflammatory, heart-healthy omega-3 essential fatty acids can be found in walnuts than in any other nut. Though they can taste a little bitter when raw, soaking them releases their tannins and allows their natural sweetness to shine through.

## Seeds

As with nuts, seeds are a very versatile ingredient. They have a variety of functions in raw desserts, from binding to thickening to replacing tree nuts. Raw seeds also contain plenty of good fats, protein, fiber, and minerals, and they should be stored in the refrigerator or freezer.

- **Chia seeds:** These unique little seeds, which come in regular (black) and white varieties, are positively packed with omega-3 fats, fiber, and protein. When combined with water, they form a mucilaginous gel, which may sound ugly, but it's seriously awesome. Chia seeds are fabulous at binding to toxins and scrubbing waste from inside your digestive tract. Ground chia seed can be used to replace ground flaxseed in recipes.

- **Flaxseeds:** Full of plant lignans, omega-3 fatty acids, and fiber, flaxseeds also become gelatinous when ground and soaked. As such, they can be used as a binder in raw recipes. The whole seeds are indigestible and must be ground before eating or using in a recipe. You can either grind your own whole flaxseed in a clean coffee grinder or buy pre-ground flax, storing it in the freezer after opening. I find flax to have a pretty strong flavor, so I only occasionally include it in my desserts.

# SOAKING NUTS AND SEEDS

In raw food prep, nuts and seeds are often soaked for multiple reasons. Some, particularly nuts with skins such as almonds, walnuts, and pecans, contain enzyme inhibitors that must be neutralized through soaking so that our bodies can more comfortably digest them. Other times, nuts and seeds are soaked for texture's sake, to allow them to soften and become easier to blend.

When a recipe calls for "1 cup nuts, soaked," simply place one cup of dry nuts in a bowl, cover with cold water, and let sit at room temperature for the amount of time indicated in the chart below. In a recipe where the nuts or seeds require soaking, the amount called for is always measured dry, before the soaking step. The soaking time need not be precise; if you only have 30 minutes to soak some cashews, for instance, just use warm water instead of cold, and place the bowl in a warm place to speed the soaking process.

| Soaking Times for Nuts and Seeds | | | |
|---|---|---|---|
| Nut/Seed | Soaking Time | Nut/Seed | Soaking Time |
| Almonds | 8 to 12 hours | Macadamia nuts | 2 to 4 hours |
| Brazil nuts | 6 to 8 hours | Pecans | 4 to 6 hours |
| Cashews | 2 to 4 hours | Pistachios | 2 to 4 hours |
| Chia Seeds | do not soak | Pumpkin Seeds | 2 to 4 hours |
| Flaxseeds | do not soak | Sesame Seeds | do not soak |
| Hazelnuts | 6 to 8 hours | Sunflower Seeds | 2 to 4 hours |
| Hempseeds | do not soak | Walnuts | 6 to 8 hours |
| **Note:** Do not soak nuts in recipes that call for dry nuts. | | | |

## Drying Soaked Nuts and Seeds Is Optional

You may also choose to soak and dry your nuts and seeds in advance to both improve digestibility and extend shelf life. Fresh nuts and seeds ought to be stored in the refrigerator to preserve their healthy fats, but soaked-and-dried ones can be stored at room temperature for up to a year.

Drying soaked nuts and seeds IS an extra step, and I want to stress that it is *completely optional*—in all recipes calling for dry nuts or seeds, you can absolutely use them straight out of the bag. That said, it takes very little effort and can be done in advance. Any time I buy raw nuts, I immediately soak and dry them before storing, so they're ready to go whenever I need them. They can always be re-soaked later for recipes calling for soaked nuts and seeds.

Simply soak the nuts or seeds for the proper amount of time as indicated in the chart above, rinse and drain them thoroughly, and transfer them to mesh-lined dehydrator trays and dehydrate at 115°F for 24 to 48 hours. To use a conventional oven, transfer them to a parchment-paper-lined baking sheet and gently bake at 200°F for about 2 hours, or until dry and crisp, stirring occasionally.

- **Hempseeds:** These superseeds have it all: essential fats, dietary fiber, complete protein, and loads of minerals. They're tiny and nutty-tasting, and I love making them into a nutritious nondairy milk (see page 27).

- **Pumpkin seeds:** A great seed to use as a tree-nut replacement, pumpkin seeds (sometimes called "pepitas") are packed with minerals like zinc and iron.

- **Sesame seeds:** I most often use these little calcium powerhouses in their ground form, called tahini (see the Oils and Butters section below).

- **Sunflower seeds:** Full of vitamin E and delicious in their own right, sunflower seeds are my go-to seed for replacing tree nuts when I need to make a recipe nut-free. See the Flours and Grains section below for information on making nut-free flour out of sunflower seeds.

## Oils and Butters

High-quality plant oils and butters can play an important role in the texture and consistency of raw pastries. Don't fear the fat—it's good for you. Nowadays, a lot of people shun oil, as it's not a whole food. Although I don't subscribe to that viewpoint, most of my dessert recipes are naturally oil-free, and the ones that aren't can almost always be made that way by swapping the corresponding butter for the oil (just check the list of substitution and variation options at the bottom of each page).

- **Coconut oil:** A superfood if there ever was one, coconut oil is extremely rich in medium-chain triglycerides—beneficial saturated fats that convert to energy instead of body fat. Lauric acid in particular (which constitutes half the total fat of coconut oil) has been found to have antimicrobial and antibacterial properties and to help raise HDL (or "good cholesterol") levels. It can also assist in weight loss and normalizing thyroid function. Coconut oil is extremely shelf-stable, and can last for a year or more without spoiling. It's semi-solid at room temperature, but should generally be melted before using. Since coconut oil's melting temperature is just 76°F, all you have to do to melt it is put it in a warm place (such as next to a window if it's warm outside, or on top of the refrigerator) for an hour or two. For faster melting, warm it in a dehydrator or partially submerge the jar in warm water.

- **Coconut butter:** First things first: coconut *oil* and coconut *butter* are two separate and very different ingredients. The oil is the pure fat that's extracted from the coconut meat, while the butter *is* the coconut meat, dried and ground into a smooth paste. That said, coconut butter can often be used in place of coconut oil, and vice versa, in my recipes. Storebought coconut butter can be extremely pricey, so see page 36 for how to make your own coconut butter inexpensively at home.

- **Almond butter:** Purchasing organic, raw almond butter from the store can be expensive, so I often make my own at home in my food processor (see pages 33-34).

- **Cashew butter:** Cashew butter is almond butter's milder, creamier cousin. Once again, I make my own from raw cashew pieces (see page 35).

- **Sunflower seed butter:** A great nut butter replacement for those on nut-free diets, roasted "sunseed" butter can be found quite affordably at health food stores or can be made (raw or roasted) at home (see page 37).

- **Tahini:** Sesame seed butter, or tahini, is a rather bitter butter most famous for its inclusion in hummus. Though its flavor can be quite assertive, I'm a big enough fan to include it in a couple recipes in this book. Raw tahini can be extraordinarily costly, so I just use roasted tahini more often than not.

- **Cacao butter:** Solid at room temperature and liquid when melted, cacao or cocoa "butter" is actually the oil extracted from cacao beans. It is an important component in everyone's favorite treat: chocolate. See the Chocolate section below for more details on cacao butter.

- **Others:** You can find oils and butters made out of just about any nut or seed nowadays. The oils don't hold much interest for me (when it comes to sweets, I'm a coconut oil and cacao butter devotee), but mention exotic treats like hazelnut butter or macadamia nut butter to me and I may start drooling. The best part is that *any* nut butter can be made at home by simply following the instructions for making almond butter (page 33) or cashew butter (page 35), substituting your favorite nut(s)!

## Chocolate

Ahh, chocolate...quite possibly the world's favorite indulgence. All chocolate comes from the pods of the *Theobroma cacao* tree. The seeds inside the cacao pod are known as cacao beans (or cocoa beans), and are the whole-food form of chocolate.

- **Cacao powder:** Cacao powder is the dried, ground solids of the cacao bean, and is simply raw, unprocessed cocoa powder. It's a surprisingly great source of minerals like calcium, magnesium, and zinc, and has become famous in recent years for its levels of flavonoids (cardio-protective antioxidants) and PEA (phenylethylamine, a mood booster). Yes, chocolate can be good for you. Cacao powder does contain stimulants in the form of caffeine and theobromine, though, so if you're extremely sensitive to stimulating substances, you may want to substitute carob powder (described below). In my recipes, you are *always* free to use regular (roasted) unsweetened cocoa powder in place of raw cacao powder.

- **Cacao butter:** Pure, raw, cream-colored cacao butter (or "cocoa butter") is the oil of the cacao bean. It is rich in vegetable-based saturated fats, largely comprised of stearic acid (which has a neutral effect on cholesterol levels) and capric acid (another healthy antiviral, antimicrobial medium-chain triglyceride). Cacao butter is what gives chocolate its heavenly aroma and melt-in-your-mouth texture. To melt it before using, shave, grate, or chop a chunk of cacao butter, either placing it in a small bowl and warming in the dehydrator, or transferring it to a double boiler and melting on the stove over *very* low heat. I store my cacao butter in the fridge.

- **Cacao nibs:** Peeled, partially ground cacao beans are called cacao "nibs." These small, crunchy, and slightly bitter nibs are like nature's own unsweetened chocolate chips!

- **Carob powder:** Made from the dried, ground pulp of carob pods, carob powder is often considered a suitable substitute for cacao powder in recipes—it doesn't really taste like chocolate, but its malty, slightly sweet flavor is something that many people come to love in its own right. It lacks the characteristic bitterness and the stimulant content of cacao; it also lacks the antioxidants and rich flavor (though it does have more calcium!). If you're a fan of carob, you can consider it interchangeable with cacao powder in my recipes.

- **Nondairy chocolate chips:** As much I enjoy making chocolate chunks from scratch (see page 166) for use in my desserts, I always have a bag or two of allergen-free nondairy chocolate chips in my pantry for those times when my freezer stash of homemade raw chocolate has run dry. There is *no* shame in going the convenient route!

## Flours and Grains

The vast majority of my recipes are entirely grain-free. I do sometimes use oats or oat flour for texture or to craft a lighter dessert. Some people are sensitive to avenin, the protein found in oats, and should avoid oats and oat flour altogether. If you follow a grain-free diet, oats and oat flour can be easily replaced or omitted in most of the recipes that contain them; simply check the list of substitution and variation options at the bottom of each page.

- **Oats:** Old-fashioned rolled oats are not raw (they're steamed when rolled), but they're widely available and perfectly suitable for my recipes. Opt for certified gluten-free oats, unless you're certain you have no sensitivity to gluten. If you do want to seek out truly-raw oat flakes, they can be purchased online, but I find them to be too bitter, so I stick with gluten-free old-fashioned rolled oats in my kitchen and recipes. Oats are an excellent source of beta-glucan, a particularly healthful type of soluble fiber.

- **Oat flour:** Oat flour can be easily made at home by grinding up old-fashioned rolled oats (see page 32), or you can purchase it in stores or online.

- **Coconut flour:** When mature coconut meat is blended in liquid and strained, the leftover solids are dried and ground into a fluffy flour. Coconut flour is indispensable in the recipes that call for it—*it cannot be replaced or substituted.* It also cannot be made at home (at least not without a ton of work), so please go ahead and purchase some now—you'll have no trouble using it up once you delve into this book. Nowadays, you can commonly find it in health food stores, but you can get it especially cheap online. Coconut flour contains an incredible amount of fiber—about 3 grams per *tablespoon!*

> ## COCONUT FLOUR IS INDISPENSABLE!
>
> Coconut flour is indispensable in the recipes that call for it—*it cannot be replaced or substituted.*

- **Almond flour:** The texture of almond flour (sometimes called "almond meal") can vary quite a bit, from soft and fine to rough and grainy. Both types can be made at home (see pages 29-30) or purchased in stores or online, and either type will work in my recipes.

- **Cashew flour:** I like using cashew flour, with its slightly sweeter flavor, in tender raw pastries like cakes. It's uncommon to find cashew flour in stores (though it's available online), but it's so easy to make yourself that I suggest you go the home-made route (see page 30).

- **Sunflour:** Sunflower seed flour, or "sunflour," as I have dubbed it, is something that is not (to my knowledge) sold anywhere, in stores or online. I created it as an ideal substitute for nut-based flours, so you'll often see it called for in nut-free variations on my desserts. Whip it up yourself at home using the instructions on page 31.

- **Others:** Seed/pseudograin flours like buckwheat and quinoa, while not necessarily raw, are high in fiber, magnesium, manganese, and protein, and either one makes a great avenin-free alternative to oat flour.

### Sweeteners

Sugar is an essential component of most desserts. It's always controversial, and, let's face it, it's also delicious! Luckily, we have a wealth of unrefined sweetener options at our fingertips nowadays.

- **Coconut nectar:** My #1 liquid sweetener of choice these days is the ambrosial amber syrup known as coconut nectar. Not only is it utterly scrumptious, it's also low on the glycemic index and chock-full of amino acids, essential minerals, and B vitamins. It's made by gently heating the sap of the coconut palm tree until it thickens and condenses to a sticky, syrupy consistency. I consider it the ideal liquid sweetener, but agave nectar is always a suitable substitute.

- **Agave nectar:** It's no secret that agave nectar has come under fire in recent years for its high fructose content and questionable level of processing. That said, it's much more widely available (and affordable) than coconut nectar, so do not hesitate to substitute it in my desserts; many of my recipe testers for this book did just that. Though I've largely abandoned its use in my own kitchen, I do still keep a bottle of organic, raw agave nectar on hand for when I need a sweetener that's thinner than coconut nectar but slightly more viscous than maple syrup. (The only recipe in this book that specifically requires agave nectar is the Baklava Blondies on page 79.)

- **Maple syrup:** Since maple syrup is the boiled sap of maple trees, it is not raw, but I use it freely in my raw dessert recipes. It's minimally processed and actually contains respectable amounts of minerals like manganese and zinc. Plus, its distinct taste is simply irreplaceable. Always buy 100% pure maple syrup (never "pancake syrup"), and stick with Grade B, which has the most robust flavor.

- **Date syrup:** Consisting of nothing but puréed dates and water, date syrup contains all the fiber and potassium of whole dates, making it a true whole-foods sweetener. It's only about two-thirds as sweet as other liquid sweeteners, so it's not a simple 1-to-1 substitution, but I'll always let you know when you can sub it in for another sweetener and how much of it to add. You'll see bottles labeled "date syrup" in stores, containing a dark substance akin to maple syrup. When I refer to it, I'm always talking about the homemade stuff, which is ridiculously simple and cheap to whip up (see page 38).

- **Coconut palm sugar:** Whether you call it coconut sugar, palm sugar, coconut crystals, or jaggery, this is one fantastic granulated sweetener. It's produced by taking the process of making coconut nectar (see above) one step further, evaporating the coconut sap until no moisture remains. Coconut palm sugar is my very favorite granulated sweetener, with its low glycemic index, high mineral and B-vitamin content, and marvelous flavor (like brown sugar with a caramel edge—divine!). You can always substitute Sucanat or date sugar if you prefer.

- **Dried fruit:** Dried fruits, especially dates and raisins, are often used as both a sweetener and a binder in raw desserts. Please see the Fruits section below for discussions on specific dried fruits.

- **Stevia:** The only all-natural, calorie-free sugar substitute currently available is *Stevia rebaudiana,* or stevia leaf. Up to 300 times sweeter than sugar, stevia leaf extract can be purchased in liquid or powdered form, as well as in packets. It can be useful for anyone desiring a low-glycemic, carbohydrate-free alternative to natural sugars, as it has no impact on blood sugar levels. Its intense sweetness and bitter aftertaste can be a turn-off for some, but once my taste buds adjusted, I became a huge fan. When sweetening to taste with stevia, always start by adding only the smallest amount possible—literally a few droplets of liquid stevia or a tiny pinch of

---

### WHY SWEETEN WITH STEVIA?

Stevia has become popular in both the raw and the non-raw food worlds, and for good reason. It has no calories and no effect on blood glucose, but is still a "natural sweetener" (it's an herb/herbal extract). As such, stevia is widely-embraced by and appealing to health-conscious bakers and eaters.

Many people are skeptical of stevia, though, and understandably so—some brands have an unpleasant aftertaste. That's why I recommend NuNaturals stevia pretty exclusively. It's got a clean, completely not-bitter flavor that no other stevia (that I've found) can compete with. It's also widely available; even my local (non-natural-foods, smaller) grocery stores carry it.

If for any reason you can't consume stevia, I have provided a Sugar Substitution Chart on page 12 that will allow you to experiment with adapting stevia-containing recipes to use different sweeteners.

the powdered form—and tasting for sweetness before adding any more (and then, again, adding only a drop or a pinch at a time). My favorite brand of stevia, by far, is NuNaturals. Once you become experienced with using stevia, you may develop a preference for a particular form of it; for example, I most often tend to use liquid stevia. Consult the Sugar Substitution Chart below to find out how to replace one type of stevia in my recipes with another type of your choice.

■ **Others:** There are a plethora of other unrefined sugars out there to check out (some raw and some not). You might explore options like yacon syrup, brown rice syrup, sorghum syrup, molasses, Sucanat, date sugar, maple sugar, lucuma powder, evaporated cane juice, or even sugar-free sweeteners like xylitol or erythritol. (Though I do not include honey in my recipes in order to keep them 100% vegan, you may substitute at your discretion.) And if all you have on hand is ordinary white or brown sugar, I don't mind one bit if you use it in these recipes!

## Fruits

Whether fresh or dried, fruit is nature's candy!

■ **Fresh fruit:** Seasonal fresh fruit is sweet, hydrating, and high in vitamins; using it to make succulent raw desserts is a no-brainer. Some fresh fruits you'll see show up in my recipes are apples, bananas, blueberries, cherries, kiwifruit, lemons and limes (for their juice), mangoes, peaches, pineapple, raspberries, and strawberries. Is your mouth watering yet?. Non-sweet avocados (yes, it's a fruit) also make a number of appearances in this book. Since so much of raw pastry-making uses

| Sugar Substitution Chart | | | | | |
|---|---|---|---|---|---|
| Coconut Nectar, Agave Nectar, Maple Syrup | Date Syrup (page 38) | Coconut Palm Sugar, Sucanat, Date Sugar, Cane Sugar | Pure Stevia Powder | Liquid Stevia | Stevia Packets |
| 2 teaspoons | 1 tablespoon | 2 teaspoons | 1/32 teaspoon | 1/4 teaspoon (10 drops) | 1 packet |
| 2 tablespoons | 3 tablespoons | 2 tablespoons | 3/32 teaspoon | 3/4 teaspoon (30 drops) | 3 packets |
| 1/4 cup | 6 tablespoons | 1/4 cup | 3/16 teaspoon | 1 1/2 teaspoons | 6 packets |
| 1/3 cup | 1/2 cup | 1/3 cup | 1/4 teaspoon | 2 teaspoons | 8 packets |
| 1/2 cup | 3/4 cup | 1/2 cup | 3/8 teaspoon | 1 tablespoon | 12 packets |
| 3/4 cup | 1 cup + 2 tbsp | 3/4 cup | 9/16 teaspoon | 4 1/2 teaspoons | 18 packets |
| 1 cup | 1 1/2 cups | 1 cup | 3/4 teaspoon | 2 tablespoons | 24 packets |

"dry" ingredients like nuts, seeds, and flours, I get particularly excited about juicy fruit-centered raw treats.

- **Dates:** Luscious, potassium-packed dates are an all-purpose staple in raw desserts, and they are my favorite whole-food sweetener. Their sticky texture can bind together brownies, bars, pie crusts, energy balls, and more. They can be blended into a syrup (see the Sweeteners section on page 11) or even a caramel sauce (page 191), or they can be munched on out-of-hand. A pitted date stuffed with a spoonful of cashew butter is one of the world's simplest – and tastiest – snacks! Semi-dry Deglet Noor dates are the most common and inexpensive variety, and they often come pre-pitted. Medjool dates are the softest, sweetest variety, and they tend to be sold with their pits still in. *Always* remove the pits from your dates before using them. My recipes call for pitted dates in cup measurements, since they can vary in size quite a bit. Generally, I've found that there are about 20 pitted Deglet Noor dates to a cup and 10 pitted Medjool dates to a cup. Many other delicious dates exist (Barhi, Halawi, Khadrawi, and honey dates are some other well-known varieties). Use whichever one you love best!

- **Raisins:** Dark (also called Thompson or Flame) raisins and golden (including Sultana and Hunza) raisins are not only excellent ingredients in their own right, they can also make an affordable and readily-available substitute for dates. When subbing raisins for pitted dates, make sure your raisins are nice and soft; dried-out ones won't work nearly as well.

- **Other:** I like to keep an assortment of other dried fruits on hand, such as apricots, cherries, cranberries, figs, and goji berries. Make sure to buy dried fruit that has no sugar added ("fruit-juice-sweetened" is okay in the case of tart fruits like cranberries), and whenever possible, opt for unsulfured varieties.

## Other

These miscellaneous items don't fit neatly into any other category, but are still important to consider.

- **Unsweetened dried coconut:** When people think they dislike coconut, it's usually chewy dried coconut that they don't enjoy. It's such a culinary chameleon, though, that even avowed coconut-phobes ought to stock it in their kitchen. Not only does it comprise the entire ingredient list of the heavenly spread known as coconut butter (page 36), it can also be used to make coconut milk (see page 28) and employed as a substitute for oats in many of my recipes. The "unsweetened" part is essential; don't buy the sugar-loaded "baking coconut" from the supermarket by mistake. Also be sure not to purchase "reduced fat" dried coconut, especially if you plan to use it to make coconut butter, as it simply won't work. I most often use unsweetened *shredded* coconut, but you can get unsweetened *flaked* coconut as well.

- **Coconut water:** Though I only use it in a couple recipes in this book, it's still a great thing to keep on hand. The best place to get refreshing, electrolyte-rich coconut water is straight out of a young Thai coconut, but there are also decent storebought options nowadays. The only kind I'll buy, though, is made by Harm-less Harvest, and is 100% raw and organic. It's so blissfully delicious, it tastes like it literally *just* came out of the coconut. One sip will transport you to the tropics!

- **Flavor extracts:** The only one you truly *need* to keep on hand is a good-quality pure vanilla extract (no "vanilla flavoring" or "imitation vanilla extract," please!). I also like to stock almond, hazelnut, coffee, coconut, and peppermint extracts.

- **Protein powder:** I lead an active lifestyle, and though I never stress over my protein intake, I do enjoy including high-quality, nondairy, hypoallergenic protein powders in my diet. I created a few recipes in this book as high-protein treats, suitable for a post-workout nosh or an after-school snack, and I suggest a protein-added varia-tion for several others. When it comes to protein powder in desserts, you should only use one that you absolutely love, as its flavor will usually be very prominent. A good rule of thumb is: if you can mix it with nothing but plain water and it still tastes great to you, it's suitable to use in recipes. If you're not into protein powder, just skip over the couple of recipes that require it.

- **Sea salt:** I firmly believe that all sweet treats taste better and brighter with a dash of salt. So as you'll see, I include small amounts of good-quality, mineral-rich sea salt in almost every recipe in this book. Any kind of natural *sea* salt is fine—just don't buy the bleached, processed stuff labeled "table salt."

- **Spices:** Ground cinnamon is the one crucial spice you should always have on hand for raw desserts. I include it in quite a few recipes for its warm, naturally-sweet flavor. I use ground turmeric sometimes to add a pleasant yellow color to lemony or banana-based sweets. Ground cardamom adds a nice touch to exotic treats like Kheer (page 152), but isn't essential.

- **Vegetables:** Naturally, you'll need carrots if you plan to make carrot cake (page 94). Fresh baby spinach leaves can be used to give extra nutrition to puddings or a pop of color to ice creams, but they are an elective addition.

## Optional

All of these ingredients can be classified as "nice to have, but not required." Pick and choose which ones you'd like to include in your pantry!

- **Coffee:** A lot of raw foodists eschew coffee, but not I. Fresh brewed coffee and/or instant coffee granules find their way into a couple of my recipes, but caffeine-avoiders can easily use coffee extract instead (check the substitutions list after each recipe).

- **Vanilla beans:** Real vanilla beans are a completely optional ingredient in my reci-pes—but they're also completely to-die-for. They can cost less than $1 apiece if you buy them in bulk, and they can be stored for a long time in your cupboard. When I blend a vanilla bean into something, I just throw in the whole bean. If you don't have a high-speed blender (or aren't quite as much of a vanilla fiend as I am), you'll want to cut a lengthwise slit in the bean and scrape out the inner seeds with the back of your knife. (Hint: stick the empty "bean skin" into a container of sugar to make homemade vanilla sugar...or into a bottle of vodka, for homemade vanilla vodka!)

- **Superfoods:** Superfoods can be fun additions to a raw pastry chef's pantry, but are not at all necessary to invest in if you don't want to. They can be expensive and hard to track down. There are several that I absolutely love – such as malty, hormone-stabilizing maca powder; nutty, mildly sweet mesquite powder; and fruity, caramel-flavored lucuma powder – but they are not required to make the recipes in this book. (In the few instances in which I suggest them, they're always optional or replaceable.) I did, however, include one recipe for the superfood fanatics out there who already stock things like açaí powder, spirulina, and dried mulberries: the Superfood Snackers on page 180!

- **Storebought staples:** In a perfect world, we'd always have a fresh batch of homemade nondairy milk in the fridge, lemons and apples on the countertop, nut butters and raw flours pre-made and ready to go, and handmade raw chocolate in the freezer...and a million dollars in the bank, and a spouse that always takes care of the laundry. Come on! This is the real world, where I might suddenly need to whip up a pie or cake for company. Or discover that my husband polished off the last of our apples. Or I might spontaneously develop an intractable craving for a warm chocolate chip cookie. It happens. In such situations, it can be invaluable to have storebought staples on hand, such as a carton of almond or coconut milk, bottled lemon juice, unsweetened applesauce, a jar of almond or coconut butter, oat flour or almond flour, or even a bag of nondairy chocolate chips. You never know when you might have a "dessert emergency," and planning ahead is, after all, the practical thing to do.

---

### WHY NO COCONUT MEAT OR IRISH MOSS GEL?

Astute raw foodies may have noticed by now that I haven't listed fresh young Thai coconut meat anywhere. Considering it's among my favorite foods on the planet, why haven't I mentioned it? It's quite simple: I wanted to make this book 100% newbie-friendly and as unintimidating as possible. It was clear to me that this meant no coconut-cracking should be required. Irish moss is another specialty ingredient that's fantastic for "lightening up" raw treats, but it can be a pain to find and work with, especially if you've never used it before. So I decided it didn't belong in these recipes either. Long story short, none of the desserts in this book call for Irish moss gel or fresh coconut meat.

That said, if you're an experienced coconut-hacker or Irish moss aficionado, I encourage you to play around with including them in these recipes. As a general rule, you can replace 1/4 to 1/3 of the soaked nuts in any purée (such as pie fillings, puddings, ice creams, or frostings) with an equal amount of chopped young coconut meat or Irish moss gel. You can also add a scoop of Irish moss gel (about 1/4 cup) to any cake or cupcake batter for a fluffier texture.

## Choosing Organic

Purchasing organic fruits, vegetables, nuts, and seeds can reduce your exposure to the pesticides, chemical additives, and genetically modified organisms (GMOs) often present in conventionally grown food products. That said, if you're working with a limited budget, buying organic is completely optional. If you'd like to be selective in your organic food shopping, my personal recommendation is to choose organic versions of the fresh fruits and vegetables that you eat or use without peeling, such as berries, cherries, and leafy greens.

## Equipment Guide

A kitchen full of expensive gadgets is not required to make delicious raw pastries; it's really very easy to get by with just a minimum of equipment. Here's what I use most often in my own kitchen, as well as some alternatives to the more obscure or costly equipment.

**Good knives.** I recommend you have one sharp, high-quality chef's knife (seven to eight inches in length) and one paring knife (about three inches in length).

**Cutting board.** Wood, bamboo, plastic, or any other kind you choose. You need a stable (and washable!) surface on which to chop ingredients like fresh fruit.

**Measuring spoons and cups.** You must have a set of measuring spoons, as well as both liquid and dry measuring cups.

**Mixing bowls, airtight storage containers, and glass (Mason) jars.** You'll need plenty of vessels in which to make and store your raw goodies, so have a variety of sizes of mixing bowls, airtight storage containers (plastic or, preferably, glass), and Mason jars on hand.

**Pans.** You can get by with just a baking sheet, an 8-inch square pan, a 9-inch pie plate, and a muffin (or mini-muffin) tin., but I also highly recommend a small (6-inch) springform pan and a 9- or 10-inch tart pan (and/or several mini tartlet pans).

**Utensils.** A vegetable peeler, whisk, and sturdy rubber spatula are all must-haves. An offset spatula, Microplane grater (for zesting), a cookie cutter or two, and a rolling pin are also nice to have.

**Strainer/colander.** A strainer or colander is good for rinsing fresh fruit or soaked nuts and seeds.

**Nut milk bag.** Helpful for making smooth, homemade nondairy milks, a nylon nut milk bag (or sprouting bag, or paint straining bag) is used to separate the pulp from the milk. If you don't plan to make homemade nut milks from scratch, though, you won't need one.

**Squeeze bottles.** You'd be shocked just how useful a couple of inexpensive plastic squeeze bottles can be in your kitchen! You can use them for piping icings or drizzling other toppings. That said, you can certainly get by without them.

**Ice cream maker.** An ice cream maker is a fun and easy way to churn up frozen treats, but it's a totally optional appliance. Only two of the ice cream recipes in Chapter 7 require it, so you'll still be able to make 98% of the recipes in this book if you don't own one!

**Food processor.** A food processor is essential for many recipes in this book. It doesn't have to be fancy—you can easily find a good one for under $100—and all you need is the basic S-blade it comes with. I have both an 11-cup model and a 3-cup mini version, but the only one you really need is the larger, standard (11- to 14-cup) size.

**Blender.** A super-powerful high-speed blender such as a Vitamix or Blendtec will transform the way you prepare food. It's definitely an investment, but it'll last a lifetime. You won't believe the dreamily smooth purées it'll turn out. That said, don't fret if you only have a more modest blender. I know many people that get by just fine with a Magic Bullet, a Ninja, or even a Tribest personal travel blender. Your purées won't be quite as silky-smooth, but they'll still taste great. When blending nuts and seeds, you may just want to soak them an extra couple hours in warm water if using a regular blender.

**Stand mixer.** A stand mixer can be a great tool for making cake batters and cookie doughs, but if you don't have one, there's no need to run out and buy one. You can just as easily use your food processor instead.

---

### ABOUT DEHYDRATING AND DEHYDRATORS

Dehydration is the process of evaporating liquid out of foods. In raw cuisine, a dehydrator is used to "bake" foods at temperatures below 118°F (48°C) in order to preserve all the nutrients, vitamins, and enzymes within. I love my Tribest brand Sedona dehydrator, but Excalibur and TSM are good brands as well. For each dehydrator tray, you'll also need a Teflex sheet, a nonstick surface on which to place wet foods until they're dry enough to transfer to mesh trays (many dehydrators come with a few of these).

Not everyone wants to invest in a dehydrator, at least not right away, so for those of you just getting started in raw food, I provide conventional oven-baking directions for any and every recipe in this book that calls for dehydration. (Alternatively, you can mimic dehydration by using your oven on its lowest (warm) setting and leaving the door cracked, although this method does waste a lot of energy.) While it's true that if you use a regular oven, your food won't be technically raw (i.e., it will be cooked above 118°F), your finished product will still be composed of all-natural, ultra-healthful fruits, nuts, and seeds—and that's more than half the battle! In fact, you may enjoy the results so much that you decide you want to add a dehydrator to your kitchen.

# Pantry List

Here's what I recommend for any budding raw pastry chef's pantry. Remember, you certainly don't need to have everything on this list to begin experimenting with raw desserts. Take inventory of your fridge and pantry, then flip though this book, keeping an eye out for ingredients you have. You're sure to find numerous things you can whip up, especially if you take note of the substitution options offered at the end of every recipe.

For more information on all of these items, see the Ingredients section beginning on page 4. If you have questions on where to purchase any of the ingredients mentioned here, visit the Resources chapter.

## Nuts
Almonds
Brazil nuts
Cashews
Hazelnuts
Macadamia nuts
Pecans
Pistachios
Walnuts

## Seeds
Chia seeds
Flaxseeds
Hempseeds
Pumpkin seeds
Sesame seeds
Sunflower seeds

## Oils and Butters
Almond butter (page 33)
Cashew butter (page 35)
Coconut butter (page 36)
Coconut oil
Sunflower seed butter (page 37)
Tahini

## Chocolate
Cacao butter
Cacao nibs
Cacao powder or unsweetened cocoa
   powder
Carob powder (optional)

## Flours and Grains
Oat flour (page 32)
Old-fashioned rolled oats
Coconut flour
Almond flour (pages 29-30)
Cashew flour (page 30)
Sunflour (page 31)
Buckwheat and/or quinoa flour (optional),
   especially if intolerant of oats

## Sweeteners
Coconut nectar and/or agave nectar
Coconut palm sugar
Pure maple syrup (grade B)
Stevia: liquid stevia, pure stevia powder,
   and/or stevia packets
Others, as desired (optional): brown rice
   syrup, date sugar, evaporated cane
   juice, maple sugar, organic white or
   brown sugar, Sucanat, yacon syrup,
   xylitol, and erythritol

## Fruits
**Fresh fruit:**
   Apples
   Avocados
   Bananas
   Blueberries
   Cherries
   Kiwifruit
   Lemons
   Limes
   Mangoes

Peaches
Pineapple
Raspberries
Strawberries
**Dried fruit:**
　Apricots
　Cherries
　Cranberries
　Dates
　Figs
　Goji berries (optional)
　Raisins (dark and golden)

## Other
Unsweetened dried coconut (shredded and/or flaked)
Flavor extracts: pure vanilla extract, plus others as desired (such as almond, coconut, coffee, hazelnut, or peppermint)
Nondairy protein powders (vanilla and/or chocolate)

Sea salt
Spices: ground cinnamon, ground turmeric (optional), ground cardamom (optional)
Vegetables: carrots and fresh spinach, as desired

## Optional
Coffee (for brewing) and/or instant coffee granules
Storebought staples:
　Bottled coconut water
　Bottled lemon juice
　Flours (such as almond or oat flour)
　Nondairy chocolate chips
　Nondairy milk (such as almond or coconut milk) and yogurt
　Jarred almond/coconut/cashew butter
　Jarred unsweetened applesauce
Superfoods, such as lucuma powder, maca powder, mesquite powder, greens powder, etc.

## Substitutions and Variations

I've made this book of raw desserts as flexible as possible by providing many substitutions for ingredients and variations on the recipes. Though you can use the substitution and variation suggestions in any combination you like, I don't recommend trying to make a recipe *"everything*-free"—i.e., combining the grain-free, lower-fat, lower-sugar, nut-free, and oil-free variations all into one. Unless your dietary restrictions absolutely require it, pick just one or two and stick to them.

## Tips and Tricks

- Line pans with plastic wrap, parchment paper, or waxed paper to make for easy removal of brownies, bars, cakes, and pies.

- Any time a recipe directs you to dehydrate, set the temperature of your machine anywhere between 105°F and 115°F (40 to 46°C).

- Dehydration times are always approximate. You may need to dehydrate a recipe for slightly more or slightly less time than is called for in the instructions, depending on which machine you have, what season of the year it is, what the temperature and humidity level outside are, at what altitude you live, and the exact water content of all your ingredients.

- For the very reasons listed above, the amount of liquid you'll need to add to doughs and batters can vary quite a bit. I always let you know you can add more, a tablespoon or so at a time, until you reach the desired consistency or texture. So don't be shy—add as much as you need.

- If you're creating a nut/seed-and-dried fruit mixture (as in some of the bars, blondies, brownies, pie crusts, energy balls, etc.) and the mixture is not sticking together as well as you'd like, simply add in another pitted date or two. Moisture levels in dates can vary quite a bit. You can and should use more (or fewer), if needed.

## Don't Forget to Play and Have Fun

To the best of my ability, I have crafted these recipes to be delectable to all palates. I present each recipe in what I consider its most delicious incarnation. However, you shouldn't hesitate to utilize the provided substitution ideas to tailor the recipe to your own liking. Even though I can't vouch for every single possible permutation of these numerous alteration possibilities, I have tested (and approved) a great number of them. Similarly, some people may be more sensitive to sugar/sweeteners than I am, in which case you should always feel free to reduce the amounts of called for. You're in charge here! I fully encourage you to play around and experiment with these recipes, according to your and your family's own tastes and preferences.

## OPTIONS GUIDE

I've provided an array of helpful option notes to aid you in navigating this book and finding the best treats to fit your needs. Each recipe will be clearly noted when it is any of the following:

**20 Minutes or Less:** These recipes can be made, with no advance prep, in about 20 minutes or less. For best results, they may require time to chill afterward, but your active time in the kitchen will be under 20 minutes.

**Baking Option:** These recipes require either dehydration or baking in a conventional oven; I always provide both options. All the remaining recipes in this book are naturally no-bake!

**Grain-Free (or Grain-Free Variation):** Oats are the only grain I include in any of my desserts, and they show up in just a handful of recipes. Nonetheless, all the naturally grain-free recipes are marked as such, and most of the oat-containing recipes come with a grain-free variation option.

**Lower-Fat (or Lower-Fat Variation):** These recipes contain fewer than 10 grams of fat per serving. Lower-fat variations are often given in case you're interested in lowering the fat content of a particular treat.

**Nut-Free (or Nut-Free Variation):** Nuts are a staple in raw desserts, but I've included several naturally-nut-free recipes as well as a plethora of recipes with nut-free variation options.

**Oil-Free (or Oil-Free Variation):** Coconut oil and cacao butter are the only extracted oils I use in raw desserts. Most of my recipes are naturally oil-free, and many of the oil-containing recipes offer an oil-free variation.

**No Added Sugars (or Lower-Sugar Variation):** Recipes marked No Added Sugars are sweetened only with stevia and dates or other dried fruit. In recipes that do contain added sugars, I frequently offer lower-sugar variations to allow you to cut out, reduce, or replace the sweeteners listed.

## COCONUTS ARE NOT NUTS!

Coconuts aren't nuts at all but actually the seeds of a drupaceous fruit. My nut-free recipes and variations often contain coconut products, because they are safe for people with peanut and tree nut allergies to consume. Confusion sometimes arises over the classification of coconut because in the U.S., it's grouped with tree nuts for food-labeling purposes. This is unfortunate, since it's not even in the same botanical family! Allergic reactions to coconut are very rare, but when they occur, it means the person has a sensitivity to coconut specifically, which is separate from (and usually not even in conjunction with) a nut sensitivity or allergy.

# Back To Basics

## Milks, Butters, Flours, Syrups

Every raw pastry chef should have a bevy of "staple recipes" in his or her kitchen arsenal, although you can certainly go the storebought route for almost all of these, if you prefer – and don't feel the least bit bad if you do. That's what being "practically raw" is all about! That said, there's something very satisfying about making your own milks, flours, butters, and even sweeteners from scratch. Not only do you get to control the raw ingredients that go into these items, you also get to tweak the final product to your liking.

Homemade nut milks are one of my favorite things in the world, with their rich, unctuous mouthfeel and superior freshness. But did you know you can also make great-tasting milk from seeds, coconuts, or oats? I even have a trick for making "instant" milk if you simply don't have time to soak any nuts or seeds. Similarly, flours can be made from nuts and seeds, and whole grains too, if you choose to include them in your diet. I make my own nut, seed, and coconut butters in my food processor and save a boatload of money that way. I've even got a whole-food sweetener (hello date syrup!) and a raw applesauce up my sleeve. I think you'll be pleasantly surprised at how easy and delicious it can be to stock your pantry with homemade ingredients.

Nut Milk (page 25)

# Basics to Make Yourself
# (or Buy Ready-Made)

**Nondairy Milks**

Nut Milk — 25

Instant Nut Milk — 26

Seed Milk — 27

Instant Seed Milk — 27

Coconut Milk — 28

Oat Milk — 28

**Flours**

Almond Flour — 29

Instant Almond Flour — 30

Cashew Flour — 30

Sunflour — 31

Oat Flour — 32

**Butters**

Almond Butter — 33

Cashew Butter — 35

Coconut Butter — 36

Sunseed Butter — 37

**Other**

Date Syrup — 38

Instant Applesauce — 39

# Nut Milk

*Nut milk is my favorite all-purpose nondairy milk. I most commonly make mine with almonds.*

1 cup nuts (any kind), soaked
  overnight and drained
5 1/2 cups filtered water
Pinch of sea salt

YIELD: ABOUT 6 CUPS

*Nutritional values will vary
depending on type of nut used;
70 to 100 calories per cup is a
good average.

• Grain-Free
• Oil-Free
• No Added Sugars

**Chef's Tip:** When making
nut milk with almonds, save
the leftover pulp to make Almond Flour (see page 29).

Combine all ingredients in a high-speed blender and blend until smooth. Strain the mixture through a nut milk bag, if desired (see instructions, page 26). (Almond or hazelnut milk will require this step, while other nut milks can be just as good unstrained.) Chill until ready to serve.

Store the milk in an airtight glass bottle or jar in the refrigerator for up to 3 days.

Coconut Milk, page 28

# Instant Nut Milk

*It happens to me all the time—I realize I'm out of milk, but I can't wait overnight to soak almonds for a new batch tomorrow. This is my instant-gratification method of making nut milk.*

1 cup filtered water
1 tablespoon almond butter
   (page 33) or cashew butter
   (page 35)

**YIELD:** ABOUT 1 CUP

**Per cup:** 78 calories, 6.9g fat
(1g sat), 2.7g carbs, 2g fiber, 3g
protein

*Nutritional values will vary
slightly depending on type of
nut butter used.

• 20 Minutes or Less
• Grain-Free
• Oil-Free
• No Added Sugars

Combine the water and nut butter in a high-speed blender and blend until smooth. (Alternatively, whisk the water and nut butter together by hand in a small bowl.) Use immediately, or store in an airtight glass bottle or jar in the refrigerator for up to 2 days.

## HOW TO USE A NUT MILK BAG

Hold a nut milk bag open over a large bowl and slowly pour your freshly-blended nut milk into the bag. Twist, squeeze, and knead the bag (with clean hands!) to extract all the milk (taking care not to spill it outside the bowl) from the pulp.

## FLAVOR ENHANCERS

If you want to jazz up your homemade nondairy milks, you can blend in any of the following: a few pitted dates, stevia (any form), coconut or agave nectar, a dash of lemon juice (to brighten the natural sweetness), vanilla extract, and/or sunflower lecithin (for creaminess).

# Seed Milk

*Seeds tend to be higher in protein and omega-3 fats than nuts, so I like to shake things up in my kitchen sometimes by making seed milk rather than nut milk. Seed-based milks are also ideal for anyone with an allergy or sensitivity to tree nuts.*

1/2 cup hempseeds, sunflower seeds, sesame seeds, or a mixture
3 cups filtered water
Pinch of sea salt

YIELD: ABOUT 3 CUPS

*Nutritional values will vary depending on type of seed used; 90 to 120 calories per cup is a good average.

• 20 Minutes or Less
• Grain-Free
• Nut-Free
• Oil-Free
• No Added Sugars

Combine all ingredients in a high-speed blender and blend until smooth. Strain the mixture through a nut milk bag, if desired (see instructions, page 26). Chill until ready to serve.

Store the milk in an airtight glass bottle or jar in the refrigerator for up to 3 days.

**Chef's Tip:** If you use sunflower seeds, I recommend soaking them for 2 to 4 hours in advance and then draining them before using. The other, smaller seeds don't require soaking.

# Instant Seed Milk

*All you need for this seed-milk-in-a-jiffy is a spoonful of calcium-rich tahini (or sesame seed butter).*

1 cup filtered water
1 tablespoon tahini

YIELD: ABOUT 1 CUP

**Per cup:** 89 calories, 8g fat (1g sat), 3.2g carbs, 1g fiber, 2.6g protein

• 20 Minutes or Less
• Grain-Free
• Nut-Free
• Oil-Free
• No Added Sugars

Combine the water and tahini in a high-speed blender and blend until smooth. (Alternatively, whisk the water and tahini together by hand in a small bowl.) Use immediately, or store in an airtight glass bottle or jar in the refrigerator for up to 2 days.

# Coconut Milk

*Since coconut is a drupe, not a nut, coconut milk is another safe alternative milk for nut-sensitive folks. (See photo page 25.)*

1 cup unsweetened shredded coconut
4 cups water or coconut water
Pinch of sea salt

YIELD: ABOUT 5 CUPS

**Per cup:** 103 calories, 10g fat (9g sat), 4g carbs, 1g fiber, 1.2g protein

Combine all ingredients in a high-speed blender and blend until smooth. Strain the mixture through a nut milk bag (see instructions, page 26) and chill until ready to serve.

Store the milk in an airtight glass bottle or jar in the refrigerator for up to 3 days.

- *20 Minutes or Less*
- *Grain-Free*
- *Nut-Free*
- *Oil-Free*
- *No Added Sugars*

# Oat Milk

*If you're in need of a low-fat made-from-scratch milk, then oat milk is for you.*

1/2 cup old-fashioned rolled oats
1 3/4 cups filtered water
Pinch of sea salt

YIELD. ABOUT 2 CUPS

**Per cup.** 74 calories, 1.5g fat (trace sat), 13.6g carbs, 2g fiber, 2.7g protein

Combine all ingredients in a high-speed blender and blend until smooth. Chill until ready to serve.

Store the milk in an airtight glass bottle or jar in the refrigerator for up to 3 days.

- *20 Minutes or Less*
- *Lower-Fat*
- *Nut-Free*
- *Oil-Free*
- *No Added Sugars*

# Almond Flour

*Dehydrate or bake the pulp left over from making almond milk to create this fine-milled, versatile flour.*

Reserved pulp from 1 batch of Nut Milk (page 25) made with almonds

*Yield and nutritional values will vary depending on how well the pulp was blended and strained; about 120 calories per 1/4 cup of flour is a good average.

- Baking Option
- Grain-Free
- Oil-Free
- No Added Sugars

**Make It Raw:** Place the strained almond pulp on a Teflex-lined dehydrator tray. Dehydrate at 110°F for 8 to 12 hours or overnight, until dry.

**Make It Baked:** Place the strained almond pulp on a parchment-paper-lined baking sheet. Bake in a preheated 200°F for 1 to 2 hours, or until dry.

When the pulp is completely dry, crumble it into flour with your hands or in a food processor.

Store in a glass jar or airtight container in the refrigerator for up to 2 months, or in the freezer for 6 months or longer.

# Instant Almond Flour

*No almond pulp on hand? No problem. Finely grind some raw almonds, and voilà—you just made almond flour!*

1 1/2 cups dry almonds

YIELD: ABOUT 1 1/2 CUPS

**Per 1/4 cup:** 137 calories, 12g fat (1g sat), 4.7g carbs, 3g fiber, 5g protein

- 20 Minutes or Less
- Grain-Free
- Oil-Free
- No Added Sugars

Place the almonds in the bowl of a food processor (or a dry-top high-speed blender) and pulse until finely ground. Be careful not to overblend, or you'll end up with almond butter. It's better to have it a little gritty than overblended.

Store in a glass jar or airtight container in the refrigerator for up to 2 months, or in the freezer for 6 months or longer.

# Cashew Flour

*Cashew flour lends a tender crumb and a little bit of natural sweetness to raw goodies. I especially like using it in cake recipes.*

1 1/2 cups dry cashews

YIELD: ABOUT 1 3/4 CUPS

**Per 1/4 cup:** 157 calories, 12.4 fat (2g sat), 8.6g carbs, 1g fiber, 5.2g protein

- 20 Minutes or Less
- Grain-Free
- Oil-Free
- No Added Sugars

Place the cashews in the bowl of a food processor (or a dry-top high-speed blender) and pulse until finely ground. Be careful not to overblend, or you'll end up with cashew butter. It's better to have it a little gritty than overblended.

Store in a glass jar or airtight container in the refrigerator for up to 2 months, or in the freezer for 6 months or longer.

# Sunflour

*Sunflower seed flour, or "sunflour," as I have dubbed it, is something that is not (to my knowledge) sold anywhere, in stores or online. It is an ideal substitute for nut-based flours. You'll often see it called for in nut-free variations on my desserts.*

**1 1/2 cups dry sunflower seeds**

YIELD: ABOUT 2 CUPS

**Per 1/4 cup:** 139 calories, 12.2g fat (1g sat), 4.1g carbs, .5g fiber, 5g protein

- *20 Minutes or Less*
- *Grain-Free*
- *Nut-Free*
- *Oil-Free*
- *No Added Sugars*

Place the sunflower seeds in the bowl of a food processor (or a dry-top high-speed blender) and pulse until finely ground. Be careful not to overblend, or you'll end up with sunseed butter. It's better to have it a little gritty than overblended.

Store in a glass jar or airtight container in the refrigerator for up to 2 months, or in the freezer for 6 months or longer.

# Oat Flour

*You don't have to have a lot of oat flour pre-made and on hand at all times—you can make it "fresh" in a matter of moments, whenever you happen to need it.*

**1 1/2 cups old-fashioned rolled oats**

YIELD: ABOUT 1 1/2 CUPS

**Per 1/4 cup:** 74 calories, 1.5g fat (trace sat), 13.6g carbs, 2g fiber, 2.7g protein

- 20 Minutes or Less
- Lower-Fat
- Nut-Free
- Oil-Free
- No Added Sugars

Place the oats in the bowl of a food processor (or a dry-top high-speed blender) and pulse until finely ground.

Store in a glass jar or airtight container in the refrigerator for up to a month, or in the freezer for 6 months or longer.

**Oats:** (top) raw oat flakes; (bottom) gluten-free old-fashioned rolled oats

# Almond Butter

*Organic raw almond butter is expensive stuff, so I've taken to making my own. This recipe is simple to make, but it does require patience—expect it to take upwards of 15 minutes for the almonds to form a smooth, creamy butter. Use it in any recipe calling for almond butter.*

**3 cups dry almonds**

YIELD: ABOUT 1 1/3 CUPS

**Per tablespoon:** 78 calories, 6.9g fat (1g sat), 2.7g carbs, 2g fiber, 3g protein

- 20 Minutes or Less
- Grain-Free
- Oil-Free
- No Added Sugars

Place the almonds into a food processor and pulse into small crumbs. Turn the machine on and let it run for about 12 to 15 minutes, stopping frequently (every 1 to 2 minutes) to scrape down the sides of the bowl with a spatula. The almond butter is ready when the nuts have released their oils and the butter is completely smooth and creamy.

Transfer to a glass jar or small container and store at room temperature for up to 2 weeks, or in the refrigerator for up to 6 months.

**1**

## TO MAKE NUT BUTTER

(1) The dry nuts are placed in the food processor. (2) Once you begin processing, the nuts will quickly turn into small crumbs. (3) As you continue processing, the crumbly nuts will begin to break down and and blend together. (4) The mixture will begin to smooth out, but will still look grainy; keep on processing. (5) The nut butter is ready when the nuts have released their oils and the mixture is completely smooth.

**2**

**4**

**3**

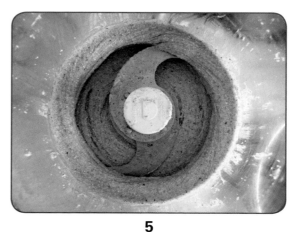

**5**

# Cashew Butter

*Cashew butter is great for when you need a nut butter with a neutral flavor and slight natural sweetness. It also takes a little less time to make than almond butter (page 33).*

**3 cups dry cashews**

YIELD: ABOUT 1 1/2 CUPS

**Per tablespoon:** 91 calories, 7.3g fat (1g sat), 5g carbs, 1g fiber, 3g protein

- 20 Minutes or Less
- Grain-Free
- Oil-Free
- No Added Sugars

Place the cashews into a food processor and pulse into small crumbs. Turn the machine on and let it run for about 10 to 12 minutes, stopping frequently (every 1 to 2 minutes) to scrape down the sides of the bowl with a spatula. The cashew butter is ready when the nuts have released their oils and the butter is completely smooth and creamy.

Transfer to a glass jar or small container and store at room temperature for up to 2 weeks, or in the refrigerator for up to 6 months.

**Chef's Tip:** Cashew butter can also be made in a high-speed blender. Blend it on high, using the tamper to push it down toward the blades. Stop every 30 seconds or so to scrape down the sides and stir the mixture to the bottom so the motor doesn't overheat.

# Coconut Butter

*Like the almond and cashew butter recipes (pages 33-35), a little patience is needed to achieve the proper silky texture for homemade coconut butter, though the process is quicker. The results are well worth the effort, and at a fraction of the price of store-bought.*

5 cups unsweetened shred-
ded coconut

YIELD: ABOUT 2 CUPS

**Per tablespoon:** 93 calories,
9.1g fat (8g sat), 3.3g carbs,
2.5g fiber, 1g protein

- 20 Minutes or Less
- Grain-Free
- Nut-Free
- Oil-Free
- No Added Sugars

Place the coconut into a food processor, turn the machine on, and let it run for 5 to 7 minutes, stopping frequently (every minute or so) to scrape down the sides of the bowl with a spatula. The coconut butter is ready when it becomes completely smooth and creamy.

Transfer to a glass jar or small container. Store at room temperature for up to 1 month, or in the refrigerator indefinitely.

**Chef's Tip:** Coconut butter can also be made in a high-speed blender. Blend it on high, using the tamper to push it down toward the blades. Stop every 30 seconds or so to scrape down the sides and stir the mixture to the bottom so the motor doesn't overheat.

# Sunseed Butter

*This nut-free butter is a suitable substitute for almond and cashew butter in many recipes.*

3 cups dry sunflower seeds

YIELD: ABOUT 1 1/2 CUPS

**Per tablespoon:** 93 calories, 8g fat (1g sat), 3.9g carbs, 1g fiber, 3.1g protein

- 20 Minutes or Less
- Grain-Free
- Nut-Free
- Oil-Free
- No Added Sugars

Place the sunflower seeds into a food processor and pulse into small crumbs. Turn the machine on and let it run for about 12 to 15 minutes, stopping frequently (every 1 to 2 minutes) to scrape down the sides of the bowl with a spatula. The sunseed butter is ready when the seeds have released their oils and the butter is *completely* smooth and creamy.

Transfer to a glass jar or small container. Store at room temperature for up to 2 weeks or in the refrigerator for up to 6 months.

**Chef's Tip:** Some people find raw sunflower seed butter to be unpleasantly bitter. If this is the case for you, simply use roasted sunflower seeds instead of raw ones. A pinch of sea salt and/or a couple teaspoons of coconut nectar or maple syrup are nice additions, too.

# Other

# Date Syrup

*My date syrup is a whole-food sweetener that can be used to replace other liquid sweeteners in many recipes. Generally speaking, 1 part coconut nectar, agave nectar, or maple syrup is equal to 1.5 parts date syrup.*

1 cup pitted dates
1 cup very warm water

**YIELD:** 10 SERVINGS (ABOUT 1 1/2 CUPS)

**Per 2 tablespoons:** 44 calories, trace fat (trace sat), 12g carbs, 1g fiber, .3g protein

- 20 Minutes or Less
- Grain-Free
- Lower-Fat
- Nut-Free
- Oil-Free

Combine the dates and water in a high-speed blender or food processor. Let sit for 15 to 20 minutes to allow the dates to soften. Turn on the machine and blend until completely smooth.

Store in a glass jar or airtight container in the refrigerator for up to 4 days.

# Instant Applesauce

*Applesauce is a common feature in my cake and cupcake recipes. If you don't have a jar of unsweetened applesauce in the cupboard, it's super-simple to make it yourself. Otherwise, feel free to use storebought in any recipes calling for applesauce.*

2 very large or 4 small red apples, peeled, cored, and chopped

**YIELD:** 4 SERVINGS (ABOUT 2 CUPS)

**Per 1/2 cup:** 51 calories, .3g fat (trace sat), 13.2g carbs, 1.5g fiber, .2g protein

- 20 Minutes or Less
- Grain-Free
- Lower-Fat
- Nut-Free
- Oil-Free
- No Added Sugars

Place the chopped apples in a high-speed blender or food processor, and blend until smooth.

Store in a glass jar or airtight container in the refrigerator for up to 3 days.

# *One Smart Cookie*

||||||||||||||||||||||||||||||||||||||||||||||||||||||||||||||||||||||||||||||||||||||||

## Cookies, Biscuits, Macaroons

Cookies are one of the most classic and simple sweet snacks you can make. You don't need servingware or utensils to eat them; they don't require refrigeration (unless you plan to store them for quite awhile), and they're completely unfussy to make. Whether they're gracing a holiday cookie tray, tucked into a lunchbox, or gobbled up while still warm, homemade cookies are a delight for kids and adults of all ages.

With no leaveners, gums, or refined flours, these raw cookies have a density and richness that baked cookies can't match. They're sturdier, heavier, and more filling than the more-processed cookies you may be accustomed to, but the beauty is that because they are more satisfying, you *can* stop at just one (only if you want to!). In my opinion, a tall, cold glass of nondairy milk (see pages 25-28) is an essential companion to any of these cookies.

In this chapter you'll find recipes for drop cookies, cutout cookies, thumbprint cookies, sandwich cookies, macaroons, shortbread, and more. Almost all have three options for preparation: dehydration, conventional oven baking, or (easiest of all!) chilling in the fridge or freezer.

Jam Thumbprint Cookies (page 58)

# Chocolate Chunk Cookies

*Chocolate chip cookies are an American classic, and with good reason—they're chewy, comforting, and studded with pockets of rich, melty chocolate. I wish I could rewind to my childhood and be greeted by a platter of these cookies and a big glass of almond milk upon arriving home from school in the afternoon!*

1 cup cashew flour (page 30)
1 cup oat flour (page 32)
1/4 cup coconut palm sugar
1/4 teaspoon sea salt
1/4 cup maple syrup
2 tablespoons water or non-dairy milk of choice (pages 25-28)
1 teaspoon vanilla extract
1/3 cup chopped Easy Chocolate Bar (page 166), frozen; or nondairy chocolate chips or chunks

YIELD: ABOUT 12 COOKIES

**Per cookie:** 158 calories, 9.6g fat (3g sat), 16.7g carbs, 1g fiber, 3.3g protein

- *Baking Option*
- *Grain-Free Variation*
- *Lower-Fat*
- *Lower-Sugar Variation*
- *Oil-Free*

In a medium bowl, combine the flours, sugar, and salt, stirring to mix. Add the maple syrup, water, and vanilla and stir vigorously until the batter comes together. Alternatively, you may mix the batter in a food processor or stand mixer. It may seem at first like there isn't enough liquid, but after a minute or more of stirring, it should come together. You can add additional water, 1 teaspoon at a time, only if absolutely needed to help the batter stick together.

**Make It Raw:** Add the frozen chopped chocolate or chocolate chips and stir to incorporate. Using a cookie scoop or a spoon, scoop the batter by rounded tablespoonfuls onto a Teflex-lined tray. Use your fingers or the bottom of a cup (moistened with water) to flatten the cookies to about 1/4-inch thick. Dehydrate at 110°F for 8 hours or overnight, until dry on the surface and slightly firmed up. The cookies will remain fairly soft.

**Make It Baked:** *Do not use the Easy Chocolate Bar if baking the cookies, as the chocolate will not hold its shape when heated.* Preheat the oven to 300°F. Add the chocolate chips or chunks and stir to incorporate. Using a cookie scoop or a spoon, scoop the batter by rounded tablespoonfuls onto a parchment-paper-lined baking sheet. Use your fingers or the bottom of a cup (moistened with water) to flatten the cookies to about 1/4 inch thick. Bake for 8 to 10 minutes, until the cookies start to look lightly browned. Let cool *completely* on the baking sheet before handling or else they will crumble.

**Make It Easy:** Add the frozen chopped chocolate or chocolate chips, and stir to incorporate. Using a cookie scoop or a spoon, scoop the batter by rounded tablespoonfuls onto a wax-paper-lined baking sheet. Use your fingers or the bottom of a cup (moistened with water) to flatten the cookies to about 1/4 inch thick. Freeze until firm.

Store the cookies in an airtight container at room temperature for up to 2 days, in the refrigerator for up to a week, or in the freezer for up to a month.

## SUBSTITUTIONS

- Cashew flour: ground walnuts, almond flour (page 29), or any other nut flour
- Oat flour: buckwheat flour or quinoa flour
- Coconut palm sugar: Sucanat, date sugar, evaporated cane juice, or organic brown sugar
- Maple syrup: coconut nectar, agave nectar, or any other liquid sweetener
- Easy Chocolate Bar/chocolate chips: carob chips or 1/4 cup cacao nibs

## VARIATIONS

- Grain-Free Chocolate Chunk Cookies: Replace the oat flour with almond flour and omit the water or nondairy milk.
- Chocolate Chocolate Chunk Cookies: Mix 1/4 cup cacao powder or unsweetened cocoa powder in with the flours and sugar. Use an additional teaspoon or two of water in the batter if needed.
- Lower-Sugar Chocolate Chunk Cookies: Replace the maple syrup with 6 tablespoons date syrup (page 38) and omit the water or milk.

# Sugar Cookie Cutouts

*These classic treats will make a stellar addition to your next holiday cookie tray. Try using cookie cutters with fun shapes, like hearts, stars, or gingerbread men.*

1 cup cashew flour (page 30)
1/2 cup coconut flour
1/4 cup coconut palm sugar
1 tablespoon ground flaxseed
Big pinch of sea salt
1/4 cup coconut nectar
1/4 cup water or nondairy
   milk of choice (pages 25-28)
1/2 teaspoon vanilla extract

YIELD: ABOUT 15 COOKIES

**Per cookie:** 98 calories, 5.2g fat (1g sat), 11.8g carbs, 2g fiber, 2.5g protein

- *Baking Option*
- *Grain-Free*
- *Lower-Fat*
- *Nut-Free Variation*
- *Oil-Free*

In a food processor or stand mixer, combine the flours, sugar, flax, and salt. Pulse together. Add the coconut nectar, water, and vanilla, and pulse until the dough forms a ball. You can add additional water or milk, 1 tablespoon at a time, if needed to help the dough stick together.

Transfer the dough onto a nonstick work surface, such as a cutting board lined with wax paper or a Teflex sheet. Use a rolling pin to roll the dough out to about 1/3 inch in thickness. Use a 2-inch cookie cutter (or simply a sharp knife) to cut rounds out of the dough; set aside. When no more cookies can be cut out, gather the dough back into a ball and roll it out again. Continue until as much of the dough is used up as possible (then snack on the last scraps!).

**Make It Raw:** Arrange the cookies on a mesh-lined tray and dehydrate at 110°F for 1 to 2 hours, until firm and dry on the surface.

**Make It Baked:** Preheat the oven to 300°F. Arrange the cookies on a parchment-paper-lined baking sheet. Bake for 7 to 8 minutes, until the cookies look dry and lightly browned. Use a spatula to move the cookies to a wire rack and let cool before handling.

**Make It Easy:** Arrange the cookies on a wax-paper-lined baking sheet and freeze until firm.

Store the cookies in an airtight container at room temperature for up to 3 days, in the refrigerator for up to a week, or in the freezer for up to a month.

**SUBSTITUTIONS**
- Cashew flour: almond flour (page 29) or any other nut flour
- Coconut palm sugar: Sucanat, date sugar, evaporated cane juice, or organic white sugar
- Flax: finely ground (white or black) chia seeds
- Coconut nectar: agave nectar, maple syrup, or any other liquid sweetener

**VARIATIONS**

- Nut-Free Sugar Cookies: Replace the cashew flour with Sunflour (page 31).
- Frosted Sugar Cookies: Decorate the finished cookies with Vanilla-Coconut Crème (page 188).
- Snickerdoodle Cutouts: Pulse 1 teaspoon ground cinnamon in with the dry mixture. Dust the finished cookies with more ground cinnamon, if desired.

# Midnight Mocha Cookies

*These dark chocolate darlings are so low-cal and low-fat, they actually would make a perfect midnight snack, but it is their deep cocoa color and flavor that gives them their name. They're also perfect for dipping into a good cup o' joe in the morning! The coffee extract is optional, but it works wonders at bringing the mocha flavor to the forefront.*

1/2 cup almond flour (page 29)
1/2 cup coconut flour
1/2 cup cacao powder
1/4 cup coconut palm sugar
1/8 teaspoon sea salt
1/3 cup very strong brewed
    coffee, plus more as needed
1/4 cup coconut nectar
1 teaspoon vanilla extract
1/2 teaspoon coffee extract
    (optional)

YIELD: ABOUT 14 COOKIES

**Per cookie:** 69 calories, 3g fat (1g sat), 11g carbs, 3g fiber, 2g protein

• Baking Option
• Grain-Free
• Oil-Free
• Lower-Fat
• Nut-Free Variation

In a food processor, combine the flours, cacao powder, sugar, and salt and pulse together. Add the coffee, coconut nectar, vanilla, and coffee extract and pulse until the dough forms a ball. Add additional coffee, 1 tablespoon at a time, as needed to help the dough stick together. The mixture will be very thick. (Alternatively, you may mix the batter in a stand mixer.)

**Make It Raw:** Using a cookie scoop or a spoon, scoop the batter by rounded tablespoonfuls onto a Teflex-lined tray. Use a fork to gently flatten the cookies to 1/3 to 1/2 inch thick, leaving fork marks in the center. (They may crack a little at the edges; that's okay.) Dehydrate at 110°F for 1 to 2 hours, flipping the cookies over halfway through, until they have firmed up slightly.

**Make It Baked:** Preheat the oven to 300°F. Using a cookie scoop or a spoon, scoop the batter by rounded tablespoonfuls onto a parchment-paper-lined baking sheet. Use a fork to gently flatten the cookies to 1/3 to 1/2 inch thick, leaving fork marks in the center. (They may crack a little at the edges; that's okay.) Bake for 8 to 9 minutes, until the bottoms of the cookies brown slightly. Use a spatula to move the cookies to a wire rack and let cool before handling.

**Make It Easy:** Using a cookie scoop or a spoon, scoop the batter by rounded tablespoonfuls onto a waxed-paper-lined plate or baking sheet. Use a fork to gently flatten the cookies to 1/3 to 1/2 inch thick, leaving fork marks in the center. (They may crack a little at the edges; that's okay.) Enjoy immediately, or refrigerate or freeze until firm.

Store the cookies in an airtight container at room temperature for up to 4 days, in the refrigerator for up to 2 weeks, or in the freezer for up to 2 months.

**SUBSTITUTIONS**

▪ Almond flour: cashew flour (page 30) or any other nut flour

- Coconut palm sugar: Sucanat, date sugar, evaporated cane juice, or organic white or brown sugar
- Coffee: water or nondairy milk plus an additional 1/2 teaspoon coffee extract or instant coffee granules
- Coconut nectar: maple syrup, agave nectar, or any other liquid sweetener

## VARIATIONS

- Nut-Free Mocha Cookies: Replace the almond flour with Sunflour (page 31).
- Double Chocolate Mocha Cookies: Pulse some nondairy chocolate chips or cacao nibs into the dough.
- No Caffeine at Midnight! Cookies: Use water or nondairy milk in place of coffee and omit the coffee extract.

# Russian Tea Cakes

*Also called Mexican Wedding Cookies or Snowballs, these tender cookies always make an appearance at my family's Christmastime gatherings.*

1 cup dry pecans
1/2 cup coconut flour
1/4 cup coconut palm sugar
Big pinch of sea salt
1/4 cup coconut nectar
2 tablespoons water or non-dairy milk of choice (see pages 25-28)
2 tablespoons coconut flour or lucuma powder

**YIELD:** ABOUT 12 COOKIES

**Per cookie:** 112 calories, 7.1g fat (1g sat), 12.3g carbs, 3g fiber, 1.6g protein

- Baking Option
- Grain-Free
- Lower-Fat
- Oil-Free

Place the pecans in a food processor and pulse until finely ground (be careful not to overprocess). Add the coconut flour, sugar, and salt, and pulse to combine. Add the coconut nectar and water or nut milk, and pulse until the dough starts to stick together, but doesn't quite form a ball. You can add additional water, 1 tablespoon at a time, if needed to help the dough come together.

Divide the dough in half, then divide each portion in half again to make 4 equal-sized portions. Divide each of the 4 portions into 3 equal-sized portions (for a total of 12 cookies). Roll each portion into a ball and flatten it just slightly so it doesn't roll around.

**Make It Raw:** Arrange the cookies on a mesh-lined tray and dehydrate at 110°F for 1 to 2 hours, until firm and dry on the surface.

**Make It Baked:** Preheat the oven to 300°F. Arrange the cookies on a parchment-paper-lined baking sheet. Bake for 11 to 12 minutes, until the cookies look dry and lightly browned. Let cool completely on the baking sheet before handling.

**Make It Easy:** Arrange the cookies on a wax-paper-lined baking sheet and freeze until firm.

When the cookies are ready, place the coconut flour or lucuma powder in a small bowl. Add one or two cookies at a time to the bowl and roll them around to lightly coat them. Repeat with the remaining cookies.

Store the cookies in an airtight container at room temperature for up to 2 days, in the refrigerator for up to a week, or in the freezer for up to a month.

## SUBSTITUTIONS

- Pecans: walnuts or almonds
- Coconut palm sugar: Sucanat, date sugar, evaporated cane juice, or organic white sugar
- Coconut nectar: agave nectar, maple syrup, or any other liquid sweetener
- Coconut flour or lucuma powder: maca powder or organic powdered sugar

# Chewy Oatmeal Raisin Cookies

*These cookies are nutritious, satisfying, and reminiscent of the ones you used to eat as a kid. The coconut oil keeps them chewy and tender.*

1 cup cashew flour (page 30)
1 cup old-fashioned rolled oats
1/2 cup oat flour (page 32)
1/4 cup coconut palm sugar
1/8 teaspoon sea salt
1/4 cup maple syrup
2 tablespoons melted coconut oil
2 tablespoons water or non-dairy milk of choice (pages 25-26)
1/2 cup raisins

YIELD: ABOUT 16 COOKIES

**Per cookie:** 128 calories, 6.4g fat (2g sat), 16.8g carbs, 1g fiber, 2.8g protein

- *Baking Option*
- *Grain-Free Variation*
- *Lower-Fat*
- *Nut-Free Variation*
- *Oil-Free Variation*

In a food processor, pulse together the flours, oats, sugar, and salt. Add the syrup, oil, and water and pulse until the batter comes together. Add the raisins and pulse a few more times to incorporate. (Alternatively, you may mix the batter in a stand mixer or by hand in a large bowl.)

**Make It Raw:** Using a cookie scoop or a spoon, scoop the batter (about 2 tablespoons per scoop) onto a Teflex-lined tray. Use your fingers or the bottom of a cup (moistened with water) to flatten the cookies to about 1/4 inch thick. Dehydrate at 110°F for 8 to10 hours or overnight, flipping the cookies over about halfway through, until dry on the surface.

**Make It Baked:** Preheat the oven to 300°F. Using a cookie scoop or a spoon, scoop the batter (about 2 tablespoons per scoop) onto a parchment-paper-lined baking sheet. Use your fingers or the bottom of a cup (moistened with water) to flatten the cookies to about 1/4 inch thick. Bake for 12 to 13 minutes, until the bottoms of the cookies start to look lightly browned. Let cool completely on the baking sheet before handling.

**Make It Easy:** Using a cookie scoop or a spoon, scoop the batter (about 2 tablespoons per scoop) onto a wax-paper-lined baking sheet. Use your fingers or the bottom of a cup (moistened with water) to flatten the cookies to about 1/4 inch thick. Freeze until firm.

Store the cookies in an airtight container at room temperature for up to 2 days, in the refrigerator for up to a week, or in the freezer for up to a month.

**SUBSTITUTIONS**
- Cashew flour: almond flour (page 29) or any other nut flour
- Oat flour: buckwheat flour or quinoa flour
- Oats: quinoa flakes or unsweetened flaked coconut
- Coconut palm sugar: Sucanat, date sugar, evaporated cane juice, or organic brown sugar
- Maple syrup: coconut nectar, agave nectar, or any other liquid sweetener

**VARIATIONS**

- Grain-Free "Oatmeal" Raisin Cookies: Replace the oat flour with almond flour and the oats with unsweetened flaked coconut. Omit the water or nondairy milk.
- Nut-Free Oatmeal Raisin Cookies: Replace the cashew flour with Sunflour (page 31).
- Oil-Free Oatmeal Raisin Cookies: Replace the coconut oil with almond butter (page 33) or coconut butter (page 36).
- Oatmeal Superfruit Cookies: Replace the raisins with dried mulberries, goldenberries, or soaked goji berries, or even less exotic dried fruits like cranberries, diced figs, or diced apricots.

# Cherry Almond Cookies

*I adore the flavor combo of cherries and almonds, and these cookies deliver it in a portable, hand-held form.*

1 cup almond flour (page 29)
1/4 cup coconut flour
1/4 cup coconut palm sugar
1/4 teaspoon sea salt
1/4 cup coconut nectar
2 tablespoons water or non-dairy milk of choice (pages 25-28)
1/4 teaspoon almond extract
1/4 cup dried cherries, roughly chopped

YIELD: ABOUT 14 COOKIES

Per cookie: 84 calories, 4.4g fat (1g sat), 11g carbs, 2g fiber, 2.1g protein

- Baking Option
- Grain-Free
- Lower-Fat
- Oil-Free

In a food processor, combine the flours, sugar, and salt and pulse together. Add the coconut nectar, water, and almond extract, and pulse until the batter becomes sticky. Add the chopped dried cherries and pulse until just combined. The dough will be very thick.

**Make It Raw:** Using a cookie scoop or a spoon, scoop the batter by heaping teaspoonfuls onto a Teflex-lined tray. Use your fingers to flatten the cookies to 1/4 inch thick. (You should end up with about 14 cookies.) Dehydrate at 110°F for 3 to 4 hours, flipping the cookies over halfway through, until firm.

**Make It Baked:** Preheat the oven to 300°F. Using a cookie scoop or a spoon, scoop the batter by heaping teaspoonfuls onto a parchment-paper-lined baking sheet. Use your fingers to flatten the cookies to 1/4-inch thick. (You should end up with about 14 cookies.) Bake for 7 to 8 minutes, until the cookies turn a light golden brown. Let cool completely on the baking sheet before handling.

**Make It Easy:** Using a cookie scoop or a spoon, scoop the batter by heaping teaspoonfuls onto a waxed-paper-lined baking sheet. Use your fingers to flatten the cookies to 1/4-inch thick. (You should get about 14 cookies.) Freeze until firm.

Store the cookies in an airtight container at room temperature for up to 2 days, in the refrigerator for up to a week, or in the freezer for up to a month.

**SUBSTITUTIONS**
- Coconut palm sugar: Sucanat, date sugar, evaporated cane juice, or organic white sugar
- Coconut nectar: agave nectar or other liquid sweetener

**VARIATION**
- Cinnamon-Raisin Cookies: Omit the almond extract, replace the chopped cherries with soft raisins, and add 1/4 teaspoon ground cinnamon.

# Nutty Buddy Sandwiches

*Between the crunchy almond bits in the cookies, the crumbly cookies themselves, and the smooth nut butter filling, you'll experience a variety of wonderful textures in every bite.*

**Cookies:**
1 cup dry almonds
1/4 cup coconut flour
1/4 cup coconut palm sugar
1/4 teaspoon sea salt
1/4 cup coconut nectar
2 tablespoons melted coconut oil

**Filling:**
1/4 cup almond butter (page 33)
2 tablespoons coconut nectar
1 teaspoon melted coconut oil
Big pinch of sea salt

YIELD: 8 SANDWICH COOKIES

**Per cookie:** 219 calories, 14.6g fat (5g sat), 19.6g carbs, 4g fiber, 4.8g protein

- *Baking Option*
- *Grain-Free*
- *Lower-Fat Variation*
- *Oil-Free Variation*

**Cookies:** Combine the almonds, coconut flour, sugar, and salt in a food processor and pulse into coarse crumbs. Add the coconut nectar and oil and pulse until the batter becomes sticky.

**Make It Raw:** Using a cookie scoop or a spoon, scoop the batter by rounded teaspoonfuls onto a Teflex-lined tray. Use your fingers to flatten the cookies to 1/4 to 1/3 inch thick. (You should end up with about 16 cookies.) Dehydrate at 110°F for 4 to 6 hours, flipping the cookies over halfway through, until they have firmed up slightly. Transfer them to the fridge for 10 to 15 minutes to firm up further before filling.

**Make It Baked:** Preheat the oven to 300°F. Using a cookie scoop or a spoon, scoop the batter by rounded teaspoonfuls onto a parchment-paper-lined baking sheet. Use your fingers to flatten the cookies to about 1/3 inch thick. (You should end up with about 16 cookies.) Bake for 7 to 8 minutes, until the cookies turn a light golden brown. Let cool completely on the baking sheet before handling (or else they will crumble).

**Make It Easy:** Using a cookie scoop or a spoon, scoop the batter by rounded teaspoonfuls onto a wax-paper-lined baking sheet. Use your fingers to flatten the cookies to 1/4 to 1/3 inch thick. (You should end up with about 16 cookies.) Freeze until firm.

**Filling:** Combine the almond butter, coconut nectar, oil, and salt in a small bowl and stir vigorously until smooth. The mixture will be thick.

When the cookies are ready, place a heaping teaspoon of the almond butter filling onto the bottoms of half the cookies. Sandwich each together with one of the remaining cookies.

Store the cookies in an airtight container at room temperature for up to 2 days, in the refrigerator for up to a week, or in the freezer for up to a month.

## SUBSTITUTIONS

- Almonds: hazelnuts, cashews, or your favorite nut
- Coconut palm sugar: Sucanat, date sugar, evaporated cane juice, or organic brown sugar
- Coconut nectar: agave nectar or any other liquid sweetener

## VARIATIONS

- Lower-Fat Nutty Buddies: Replace 1/3 cup of the almonds with old-fashioned rolled oats.
- Oil-Free Nutty Buddies: Replace the oil in the cookies with coconut butter (page 36). Replace the oil in the filling with water, OR use agave nectar in place of coconut nectar and omit the oil.
- Chocolate Nutty Buddies: Add 2 to 3 tablespoons cacao powder or unsweetened cocoa powder to the cookie dough (plus a teaspoon or two of water or nondairy milk, if needed).
- Peanut Buddies: If you're not sensitive to peanuts or overly concerned with "rawness," you can replace the almonds and almond butter with peanuts and peanut butter, respectively.

Chocolate Walnut Drop Cookies (page 57)

Protein Crinkle Cookies (page 63)

# Chocolate Walnut Drop Cookies

*The original version of this generations-old cookie recipe comes from my mom's side of the family, the Lichtenauers. We like to use black walnuts in these cookies, but you can certainly use plain walnuts if that's what you have, or substitute pecans.*

1 1/3 cups dry walnuts
1/2 cup coconut flour
1/3 cup cacao powder
1/3 cup coconut palm sugar
1/8 teaspoon sea salt
1/4 cup maple syrup
2 tablespoons water or non-dairy milk of choice (pages 25-28)
1 teaspoon vanilla extract

YIELD: ABOUT 14 COOKIES

**Per cookie:** 123 calories, 8.3g fat (1g sat), 12.5g carbs, 3g fiber, 2.7g protein

- *Baking Option*
- *Grain-Free*
- *Lower-Fat*
- *Oil-Free*

Place the walnuts in a food processor and pulse a few times, until the nuts are crushed but still chunky. Transfer 1/3 cup of the crushed nuts to a small bowl and set aside.

To the remaining crushed walnuts in the food processor, add the flour, cacao powder, sugar, and salt, and pulse together. Add the maple syrup, water, and vanilla, and pulse until the dough begins to form a ball. Add additional water or milk, 1 tablespoon at a time, as needed to help the dough stick together. Add the reserved crushed walnuts and pulse until just incorporated. The dough will be very thick.

**Make It Raw:** Using a cookie scoop or spoon, scoop the dough by rounded tablespoonfuls onto a Teflex-lined tray. Use the palm of your hand to gently flatten the cookies into a dome shape. Dehydrate at 110°F for about 2 hours, flipping the cookies halfway through, until they are firmed up.

**Make It Baked:** Preheat the oven to 300°F. Using a cookie scoop or spoon, scoop the dough by rounded tablespoonfuls onto a parchment-paper-lined baking sheet. Use the palm of your hand to gently flatten the cookies into a dome shape. Bake for 8 to 9 minutes, until the bottoms brown slightly. Use a spatula to transfer to a wire rack to cool before handling.

**Make It Easy:** Using a cookie scoop or spoon, scoop the dough by rounded tablespoonfuls onto a waxed-paper-lined baking sheet. Use the palm of your hand to flatten the cookies into a dome shape. Refrigerate or freeze until firm.

Store the cookies in an airtight container at room temperature for up to 5 days, in the refrigerator for up to 2 weeks, or in an airtight container in the freezer for up to 2 months.

### SUBSTITUTIONS

- Coconut palm sugar: Sucanat, date sugar, evaporated cane juice, or organic white or brown sugar
- Cacao powder: unsweetened cocoa powder or carob powder
- Maple syrup: coconut nectar, agave nectar, or other liquid sweetener

# Jam Thumbprint Cookies

*This is a great recipe to make with kids—they'll love pressing their little thumbs into the cookie dough balls to create tiny "bowls" to hold the jam. If you don't want to make your own Fruity Chia Jam (page 196), feel free to use any storebought jelly, jam, or preserves that you like.*

1 cup almond flour (page 29)
1/3 cup coconut flour
1/8 teaspoon sea salt
1/3 cup coconut nectar
1/4 cup water or nondairy milk of choice (pages 25-28)
1 teaspoon vanilla extract
2 tablespoons melted coconut oil
2 tablespoons coconut palm sugar, for rolling
1/2 batch Fruity Chia Jam (page 196), either version and any variation

YIELD: ABOUT 10 COOKIES

**Per cookie:** 159 calories, 9.2g fat (3g sat), 18g carbs, 4g fiber, 3.4g protein

- Baking Option
- Grain-Free
- Lower-Fat
- Nut-Free Variation
- Oil-Free Variation

In a food processor, combine the flours and salt, and pulse together. Add the coconut nectar, water, and vanilla, and pulse until combined. Add the coconut oil and pulse again until the dough is crumbly but sticks together when pressed.

Place the coconut palm sugar in a small bowl.

**Make It Raw:** Using a cookie scoop or a spoon, scoop the batter by rounded tablespoonfuls onto a Teflex-lined tray. One by one, pick up the cookies and roll them around in the small bowl of coconut sugar until the exteriors are lightly coated, then place them back onto the tray. Gently press your thumb into the center of each cookie, leaving a bowl-like indentation. Spoon about 1/2 teaspoon Fruity Chia Jam into the cavity of each cookie. Dehydrate at 110°F for 5 to 6 hours, until the cookies have firmed up slightly.

**Make It Baked:** Preheat the oven to 300°F. Using a cookie scoop or a spoon, scoop the batter by rounded tablespoonfuls onto a parchment-paper-lined baking sheet. One by one, pick up the cookies and roll them around in the small bowl of coconut sugar until the exteriors are lightly coated, then place them back onto the baking sheet. Gently press your thumb into the center of each cookie, leaving a bowl-like indentation. Spoon about 1/2 teaspoon Fruity Chia Jam into the cavity of each cookie. Bake for 10 to 12 minutes, until the bottoms of the cookies brown slightly. Use a spatula to move the cookies to a wire rack and let cool before handling.

**Make It Easy:** Using a cookie scoop or a spoon, scoop the batter by rounded tablespoonfuls onto a waxed-paper-lined baking sheet. One by one, pick up the cookies and roll them around in the small bowl of coconut sugar until the exteriors are lightly coated, then place them back onto the baking sheet. Gently press your thumb into the center of each cookie, leaving a bowl-like indentation. Spoon about 1/2 teaspoon Fruity Chia Jam into the cavity of each cookie. Refrigerate or freeze until firm.

Store the cookies in an airtight container at room temperature for up to 3 days or in the refrigerator for up to 1 week.

**SUBSTITUTIONS**

- Almond flour: cashew flour (page 30) or any other nut flour
- Coconut nectar: maple syrup, agave nectar, or any other liquid sweetener
- Coconut palm sugar: Sucanat, date sugar, evaporated cane juice, or organic white sugar
- Fruity Chia Jam: your favorite storebought all-fruit jam

**VARIATIONS**

- Nut-Free Jam Cookies: Replace the almond flour with Sunflour (page 31).
- Oil-Free Jam Cookies: Replace the coconut oil with coconut butter (page 36) or almond butter (page 33).
- Chocolate Thumbprint Cookies: Dehydrate or bake the cookies before spooning in any filling, then replace the Fruity Chia Jam (page 196) with Sugar-Free Chocolate Ganache (page 194).

# Pecan Shortbread Cookies

*These crisp on the outside, tender on the inside cookies were a consistent favorite among my recipe testers. With only four ingredients, you could practically make these with your eyes closed!*

2 cups dry pecans
1/4 cup coconut flour
1/2 teaspoon sea salt
1/2 cup maple syrup

YIELD: ABOUT 12 COOKIES

**Per cookie:** 168 calories, 13.2g fat (1g sat), 13.1g carbs, 3g fiber, 2g protein

- Baking Option
- Grain-Free
- Lower-Fat Variation
- Oil-Free

Place the pecans in a food processor and pulse until the nuts are finely ground. Do not to overprocess. Add the coconut flour and salt, and pulse to combine. Add the maple syrup, and pulse until the dough starts to stick together.

**Make It Raw:** Using a cookie scoop or a spoon, scoop the batter by rounded tablespoonfuls onto a Teflex-lined tray. Use the palm of your hand to gently flatten the cookies to about 1/3 inch thick. Dehydrate at 110°F for about 4 hours, carefully flipping the cookies over onto a mesh-lined tray halfway through, until they feel dry and firm.

**Make It Baked:** Preheat the oven to 300°F. Using a cookie scoop or a spoon, scoop the batter by rounded tablespoonfuls onto a parchment-paper-lined baking sheet. Use the palm of your hand to gently flatten the cookies to about 1/3 inch thick. Bake for 9 to 11 minutes, until the cookies are dry on top. Let cool completely on the baking sheet before handling (or else they will crumble).

Store the cookies in an airtight container at room temperature for up to 2 days, in the refrigerator for up to a week, or in the freezer for up to a month.

**SUBSTITUTIONS**
- Pecans: walnuts
- Maple syrup: coconut nectar, agave nectar, or any other liquid sweetener

**VARIATION**
- Lower-Fat Pecan Shortbread Cookies: Replace 1/2 cup of the pecans with old-fashioned rolled oats.

Pecan Shortbead Cookies (opposite)

Detox Macaroons (page 62)

# Detox Macaroons

*These melt-in-your-mouth morsels are the signature treat of my friend Megan, the Detoxinista (detoxinista.com). She developed these buttery little coco-babies as a nut-free, detox-friendly raw snack, and they are easily the best macaroons I have ever tried. They'll keep for weeks (or longer!) in the fridge or freezer, but good luck making them last that long.*

1 cup coconut butter (page 36)
3/4 cup maple syrup
1 1/2 teaspoons vanilla extract
1/4 teaspoon sea salt
2 cups unsweetened shredded coconut

YIELD: 32 MACAROONS

**Per macaroon:** 100 calories, 7.8g fat (7g sat), 7.9g carbs, 2g fiber, .8g protein

- *Baking Option*
- *Grain-Free*
- *Lower-Fat Variation*
- *Nut-Free*
- *Oil-Free*

In a large bowl, combine together the coconut butter, maple syrup, vanilla, and salt, stirring until smooth. Add the shredded coconut and stir until combined.

**Make It Raw:** Using a cookie scoop or a spoon, scoop the batter by rounded teaspoonfuls onto a Teflex-lined tray and dehydrate at 110°F for 24 to 36 hours, until the macaroons are dry on the outside.

**Make It Baked:** Preheat the oven to 300°F. Using a cookie scoop or a spoon, scoop the batter by rounded teaspoonfuls onto a parchment-paper-lined baking sheet. Bake for 22 to 25 minutes, until the macaroons are dry on the outside (the insides will remain moist). Let cool completely on the baking sheet before handling.

Store the cookies in an airtight container at room temperature for up to 5 days, in the refrigerator for up to 2 weeks, or in the freezer for 2 months or more.

**SUBSTITUTION**
- Maple syrup: coconut nectar, agave nectar, or any other liquid sweetener

**VARIATIONS**
- Lower-Fat Macaroons: Replace 1 cup of the shredded coconut with 1 cup old-fashioned rolled oats (pulsed in a food processor first until coarsely ground). Alternatively, replace one or both cups of the shredded coconut with reduced-fat unsweetened shredded coconut.
- Almond Macaroons: Replace 1/2 teaspoon of the vanilla extract with almond extract.
- Chocolate-Dipped Macaroons: Dip the dehydrated/baked macaroons into Sugar-Free Chocolate Ganache (page 194), set on waxed paper or a Teflex sheet, and refrigerate until the chocolate is set. Alternatively, drizzle the ganache on top of the macaroons.
- Lemon Kiss Macaroons: Add 1 to 2 teaspoons lemon zest to the batter.

# Protein Crinkle Cookies

*Mix 'em, mold 'em, and chill 'em—that's all the work that's required to make these low-carb, protein-packed treats. You'll definitely want to use a protein powder that you love the taste of on its own, as its flavor will be front and center in these cookies.*

2/3 cup chocolate-flavored nondairy protein powder of choice
2 tablespoons carob powder
1 tablespoon maca powder
1 tablespoon mesquite powder
1/2 cup melted coconut oil
1/2 to 3/4 cup water
10 to 15 drops liquid stevia (or equivalent sweetener of choice; see page 12), or to taste (optional)
1 tablespoon coconut flour or lucuma powder (optional)

YIELD: ABOUT 10 COOKIES

**Per cookie:** 128 calories, 11.3g fat (9g sat), 3.6g carbs, 1g fiber, 5g protein

- *20 minutes or less*
- *Grain-Free*
- *No Added Sugars*

In a large bowl, combine the protein powder, carob, maca, and mesquite, and stir to combine. Add the coconut oil and 1/2 cup water, and stir vigorously until the mixture becomes uniformly moist. Depending on what type of protein powder you use, you may need to add up to 1/4 cup more water, a tablespoon at a time, until the mixture is moist. Taste for sweetness and add stevia if desired.

With your hands, scoop up a heaping tablespoonful of the batter and gently form it into a disc shape. (The batter will be delicate and will fall apart easily, so handle it gingerly.) Place the formed cookie onto a waxed-paper-lined plate or baking sheet. Repeat with the remaining batter. Refrigerate the cookies for about 30 minutes, until firm.

When the cookies have firmed up, lightly dust the tops with the coconut flour or lucuma powder, if desired, for a "crinkle" effect.

Store the cookies in an airtight container in the refrigerator for up to 2 weeks or in the freezer for up to 2 months. If storing in the freezer, set the cookies out at room temperature for 10 to 20 minutes before eating.

**SUBSTITUTIONS**
- Carob powder: cacao powder or unsweetened cocoa powder
- Maca powder: additional carob, cacao, mesquite, or protein powder
- Mesquite powder: additional carob, cacao, maca, or protein powder
- Coconut flour or lucuma powder: organic powdered sugar or additional maca powder

**VARIATION**
- Pick-Your-Flavor Protein Cookies: Add 1/2 to 1 teaspoon of your favorite flavor extract. Try vanilla, almond, hazelnut, coffee, or peppermint!

# A Girl Walks Into a Bar...

## Bars, Brownies, Blondies

Who doesn't love a good bar? I've always appreciated the ease and simplicity of mixing a few ingredients together, throwing it into a pan, and calling it a day. Gotta love one-bowl recipes. Perfect for an after-school snack or a potluck dessert, bars are one of my favorite types of confections to make, teach, and share.

Built on a base of nuts and dried fruit, my raw bar recipes go above and beyond to offer a selection of flavor profiles and combinations to choose from. Chocoholics won't be disappointed in my cocoa-tastic brownies, and I expand my repertoire of blondies (my signature chocolate-less brownies) here with some particularly creative varieties.

In this chapter you'll discover a whole range of mouthwatering bars, from brownies and blondies to energy bars, granola bars, layered bars, and candy bars. Most of these recipes are completely no-bake and take less than 20 minutes to prepare, and they'll last for weeks in the fridge or freezer.

Goji Berry Granola Bars (page 80)

# Ultimate Raw Brownies

*I think the title says it all here. These dark chocolate brownies are love at first bite.*

1 1/2 cups dry pecans
1 cup dry walnuts
1/2 cup cacao powder
1/4 cup coconut palm sugar
1 teaspoon vanilla extract
1/8 teaspoon sea salt
1 heaping cup pitted dates
1/2 batch Sugar-Free Chocolate Ganache (page 194)

YIELD: 16 SERVINGS

**Per serving:** 218 calories, 17.9g fat (6g sat), 16.6g carbs, 4g fiber, 3.1g protein

- *20 Minutes or Less*
- *Grain-Free*
- *Lower-Fat Variation*
- *Lower-Sugar Variation*

In a food processor, combine the pecans, walnuts, cacao powder, sugar (if using), vanilla, and salt. Pulse until the nuts are finely ground (be careful not to overprocess). Add the dates, 2 to 3 at a time, pulsing between additions until each date is well-incorporated and the mixture is sticky. You can add water, 2 teaspoons at a time, if needed to help it come together. Press the mixture firmly and evenly into an 8- or 9-inch square baking pan (lined with plastic wrap for easy removal, if desired) and place in the freezer to chill while you prepare the Sugar-Free Chocolate Ganache.

Remove the pan from the freezer and pour the ganache icing over the brownies, tilting the pan to spread it around evenly. Serve immediately (they'll be delightfully oozy!) or refrigerate until ready to cut and serve.

Store the brownies in an airtight container in the refrigerator for up to a week or in the freezer for up to a month. You can eat them cold or bring them to room temperature before serving.

## SUBSTITUTIONS

- Pecans: additional walnuts, or almonds or Brazil nuts
- Walnuts: additional pecans, or almonds or Brazil nuts
- Cacao powder: unsweetened cocoa powder or carob powder
- Coconut palm sugar: Sucanat, date sugar, evaporated cane juice, or organic white or brown sugar
- Dates: soft raisins
- Sugar-Free Chocolate Ganache: Fluffy Chocolate Frosting (page 189) or Fat-Free Chocolate Syrup (page 195)

## VARIATIONS

- Lower-Fat Brownies: Replace 1/2 cup of the pecans with old-fashioned rolled oats. For the icing, use Fat-Free Chocolate Syrup (page 195) instead of the Sugar-Free Chocolate Ganache.
- Lower-Sugar Brownies: Omit the coconut palm sugar and add a couple of extra dates or a few drops of stevia, if desired.
- Caramel-Topped Brownies: Frost the brownies with Ooey Gooey Caramel Sauce (page 191) instead of the Sugar-Free Chocolate Ganache.

# Banana Butter Brownies

*These naturally-sweetened brownies make use of the magical combination of banana and chocolate. If your bananas are super-ripe and sweet, you probably won't need to add any stevia at all. Serve straight from the freezer so they don't fudge up your fingers and clothes!*

1 cup dry walnuts
1 cup dry pecans
2 medium, very ripe bananas, peeled and chopped
1/2 cup pitted dates, soaked in warm water for 15 minutes and drained
1 teaspoon lemon juice
1 teaspoon vanilla extract
1/8 teaspoon sea salt
1/3 cup cacao powder
2 heaping tablespoons coconut flour
Stevia to taste (optional)

YIELD: 12 SERVINGS

**Per serving**: 171 calories, 13.4g fat (1g sat), 13.8g carbs, 3g fiber, 3.1g protein

- *Grain-Free*
- *Lower-Fat Variation*
- *Oil-Free*
- *No Added Sugars*

In a food processor, combine the walnuts and pecans and pulse until finely ground (be careful not to overprocess). Transfer the ground nuts to a medium bowl and set aside.

In the same food processor (no need to wash it in between), combine the bananas, dates, lemon juice, vanilla, and salt. Blend until smooth, stopping to scrape down the sides if necessary. This is the "banana butter" in the title. Add the cacao powder and coconut flour and pulse until incorporated. Add the reserved ground nuts and pulse until the batter comes together. Taste for sweetness and add stevia if desired, pulsing until just incorporated. The mixture will be very sticky.

Transfer the batter to an 8-inch square baking pan (lined with plastic wrap for easy removal, if desired) and use a spatula to spread it evenly. Freeze the brownies for at least 4 hours or overnight before slicing. Allow them to thaw for 5 to 10 minutes at room temperature or 20 to 30 minutes in the refrigerator before eating.

Store the brownies in an airtight container in the freezer for up to 1 month.

## SUBSTITUTIONS
- Walnuts: additional pecans, or almonds or Brazil nuts
- Pecans: additional walnuts, or almonds or Brazil nuts
- Dates: soft raisins
- Cacao powder: unsweetened cocoa powder or carob powder

## VARIATION
- Lower-Fat Banana Brownies: Replace 1/2 cup of either the pecans or the walnuts with old-fashioned rolled oats.

# Tuxedo Cheesecake Brownies

*These black-and-white bars contain a layer of silken cheesecake filling sandwiched inside a rich, sticky brownie. When frozen, they can be picked up and eaten out of hand, while at room temperature, they're decadently gooey. You will hardly believe these are sugar-free!*

**Brownie Layers:**
1 cup dry pecans
1 cup dry walnuts
1/3 cup cacao powder
1/8 teaspoon sea salt
3/4 cup pitted dates

**Cheesecake Layer:**
1 cup cashews, soaked for 2
    to 4 hours and drained
1/4 cup water or nondairy
    milk of choice (pages 25-28)
2 tablespoons melted coco-
    nut oil
2 tablespoons lemon juice
1/2 teaspoon vanilla extract
1/8 teaspoon sea salt
30 drops liquid stevia (or
    equivalent sweetener of
    choice; see page 12), or to
    taste

YIELD: 16 SERVINGS

**Per serving:** 189 calories, 15.6g fat (3g sat), 12.5g carbs, 3g fiber, 4g protein

• *Grain-Free*
• *Lower-Fat Variation*
• *Oil-Free Variation*
• *No Added Sugars*

**Brownie Layers:** In a food processor, combine the pecans, walnuts, cacao powder, and salt and pulse until finely ground (be careful not to overprocess). Add the dates, 2 to 3 at a time, pulsing between additions until each date is well-incorporated and the mixture is sticky. Taste for sweetness, and add another date or some stevia if desired.

Press *half* of the mixture (about 1 heaping cup) firmly and evenly into an 8-inch square baking pan (lined with plastic wrap for easy removal, if desired). Place the pan in the freezer to chill. Set the other half of the mixture aside while you make the cheesecake layer.

**Cheesecake Layer:** In a high-speed blender, combine the cashews, water, coconut oil, lemon juice, vanilla, salt, and stevia and blend until smooth. You can add more water, a teaspoon at a time, as needed to help the mixture blend. Taste for sweetness and add more stevia if desired.

Remove the pan from the freezer and transfer the cheesecake mixture onto the brownie layer, spreading it evenly with a spoon or spatula. Place the pan back in the freezer for 1 to 2 hours to allow the cheesecake layer to firm up. Once frozen, remove the pan from the freezer again, and evenly scatter the remaining half of the brownie mixture on top of the cheesecake layer. Gently but firmly press the brownie bits into the cheesecake. You may still be able to see the cheesecake layer underneath; that's ok. Place in the refrigerator for at least 2 hours before cutting and serving.

Store the brownies in an airtight container in the refrigerator for up to a week or in the freezer for up to a month. Though best served cold, straight from the fridge, you can bring them to room temperature before serving if you prefer; you just may need to eat them with a fork instead of your hands!

## SUBSTITUTIONS

- Pecans: additional walnuts, or macadamia nuts or almonds
- Walnuts: additional pecans, or almonds or Brazil nuts
- Cacao powder: unsweetened cocoa powder or carob powder
- Dates: soft raisins
- Cashews: macadamia nuts

## VARIATIONS

- Lower-Fat Cheesecake Brownies: Replace 1/2 cup of the walnuts with old-fashioned rolled oats. Replace 1/4 cup of the cashews in the cheesecake layer with plain or vanilla nondairy yogurt.
- Oil-Free Cheesecake Brownies: Replace the coconut oil in the cheesecake layer with coconut butter, adding extra water if needed to blend the mixture smoothly.
- Raspberry Cheesecake Brownies: Replace the water in the cheesecake layer with Raspberry Coulis (page 192), raspberry purée, or raspberry jam.
- Cheesecake-Stuffed Blondies: Use the recipe for Famous Five-Minute Blondies II (page 73) in place of the brownie layer recipe above.

# Famous Five-Minute Blondies II

*The Famous Five-Minute Blondies in* Practically Raw *are without a doubt my most popular recipe of all time, with their seamless, chewy marriage of nuts, palm sugar, tender dates, and a kiss of sea salt. I gave my signature dessert a slight makeover here, mixing up the nuts for an even more craveworthy flavor. They're every bit as life-changing as the originals.*

2 1/2 cups dry mixed nuts, such as a combination of macadamias, walnuts, pecans, and cashews
1/4 cup coconut palm sugar
2 teaspoons vanilla extract
1/8 teaspoon sea salt
1 cup pitted dates

YIELD: 16 SERVINGS

**Per serving**: 172 calories, 12.9g fat (2g sat), 14.3g carbs, 2g fiber, 2.7g protein

- 20 Minutes or Less
- Grain-Free
- Lower-Fat Variation
- Oil-Free
- Lower-Sugar Variation

In a food processor, combine the nuts, sugar, vanilla, and salt. Pulse until the nuts are finely ground (be careful not to overprocess). Add the dates, 2 to 3 at a time, pulsing between additions until each date is well-incorporated and the mixture is sticky. Press the mixture firmly and evenly into an 8-inch square baking pan (lined with plastic wrap for easy removal, if desired). Enjoy immediately (though they will be a little fragile) or place the pan in the refrigerator or freezer to chill for a couple hours before cutting and serving (recommended).

Store the blondies in an airtight container in the refrigerator for up to 2 weeks or in the freezer for up to 2 months. They are best served chilled.

## SUBSTITUTIONS
- Coconut palm sugar: Sucanat, date sugar, or organic brown sugar
- Dates: soft golden raisins

## VARIATIONS
- Lower-Fat Blondies: Replace 1/2 to 3/4 cup of the nuts (any kind) with old-fashioned rolled oats.
- Lower-Sugar Blondies: Omit the coconut palm sugar. You may find them sweet enough as-is. And if not, simply add stevia or additional dates to taste.

# Strawberry Blondies

*These blushing beauties are one of my favorite twists on my "traditional" raw blondie bars. You must specifically seek out freeze-dried strawberries, which are crisp and light-as-air, not squishy or chewy.*

1 cup dry cashews
1 cup dry macadamia nuts
1 teaspoon lemon juice
1 teaspoon vanilla extract
1/8 teaspoon sea salt
3/4 cup pitted dates
1 ounce freeze-dried strawberries, lightly crushed

**YIELD: 12** SERVINGS

**Per serving**: 183 calories, 13.7g fat (2g sat), 14.9g carbs, 2g fiber, 3.3g protein

• *20 Minutes or Less*
• *Grain-Free*
• *Lower-Fat Variation*
• *Oil-Free*
• *No Added Sugars*

In a food processor, combine the cashews, macadamia nuts, lemon juice, vanilla, and salt. Pulse until the nuts are finely ground (be careful not to overprocess). Add the dates, 2 to 3 at a time, pulsing between additions until each date is well-incorporated and the mixture is sticky. Add the freeze-dried strawberries and pulse several more times to combine. Bits of strawberry should still be clearly visible. Press the mixture firmly and evenly into an 8-inch square baking pan (lined with plastic wrap for easy removal, if desired). Enjoy immediately or place in the refrigerator to chill for at least 2 hours before cutting and serving.

Store the blondies in the refrigerator for up to a week or in the freezer for up to a month.

## SUBSTITUTIONS
■ Cashews: additional macadamia nuts
■ Macadamia nuts: additional cashews
■ Dates: soft golden raisins

## VARIATIONS
■ Lower-Fat Strawberry Blondies: Replace 1/2 cup of the cashews with old-fashioned rolled oats.
■ Fruity Blondies: You can replace the strawberries here with any other variety of freeze-dried fruit you like—try mango or pineapple!

# White Chocolate Macadamia Nut Blondies

*My favorite type of cookie is white chocolate macadamia nut, but my favorite dessert is raw blondies, so I channeled the cookie in creating these fragrant, addictive bars.*

**Blondies:**
1 1/2 cups dry macadamia nuts
1 cup dry cashews
1/4 cup coconut palm sugar
1 teaspoon vanilla extract
1/8 teaspoon sea salt
1 cup pitted dates

**White Chocolate Glaze:**
2 tablespoons melted cacao butter
2 tablespoons maple syrup
1/2 teaspoon vanilla extract

YIELD: 16 SERVINGS

**Per serving:** 203 calories, 15.3g fat (3g sat), 16.9g carbs, 2g fiber, 2.8g protein

• *Grain-Free*
• *Lower-Fat Variation*
• *Lower-Sugar Variation*

**Chef's Tip:** If you pre-melt your cacao butter, this recipe comes together in well under 20 minutes.

**Blondies:** Combine the macadamia nuts, cashews, sugar, vanilla, and salt in a food processor. Pulse until the nuts are finely ground (be careful not to overprocess). Add the dates, 2 to 3 at a time, pulsing between additions until each date is well-incorporated and the mixture is sticky. Press the mixture firmly and evenly into an 8-inch square baking pan (lined with plastic wrap for easy removal, if desired). Place the pan in the refrigerator to chill while you make the glaze.

**Glaze:** Whisk the cacao butter, maple syrup, and vanilla together in a small bowl. With a pastry brush or a large spoon, spread the glaze evenly across the top of the blondies. Place the pan in the refrigerator to chill for at least 2 hours before cutting and serving.

Store the blondies in an airtight container in the refrigerator for up to 2 weeks or in the freezer for up to 2 months. Serve chilled, straight from the fridge.

## SUBSTITUTIONS
- Nuts: any combination of macadamia nuts, cashews, and/or pecans totaling 2 1/2 cups
- Coconut palm sugar: Sucanat or organic brown sugar
- Dates: soft golden raisins
- Maple syrup: coconut nectar, agave nectar, or any other liquid sweetener

## VARIATIONS
- Lower-Fat Macnut Blondies: Replace 1/2 cup of the macadamia nuts with old-fashioned rolled oats.
- Lower-Sugar Macnut Blondies: Omit the coconut palm sugar in the blondies and add a couple of extra dates or a few drops of stevia, if desired.

White Chocolate Macadamia Nut Blondies (opposite)

Pecan Chai Spice Bars (page 85)

# Baklava Blondies

*Baklava is among my favorite desserts of all time, but it can be messy and time-consuming to make. Raw baklava blondies to the rescue!*

1 cup dry walnuts
1 cup dry pistachios
1/2 cup dry almonds
1/4 cup coconut flour
1/8 teaspoon sea salt
1/2 cup soft golden raisins
2/3 cup pitted dates
2 tablespoons agave nectar

YIELD: 16 SERVINGS

**Per serving**: 161 calories, 10.4g fat (1g sat), 16.1g carbs, 4g fiber, 4.2g protein

- 20 Minutes or Less
- Grain-Free
- Lower-Fat Variation
- Oil-Free
- Lower-Sugar Variation

**Chef's Tip:** This is one instance in which I specifically call for agave nectar, as I find it has a honey-like flavor. You can, as always, substitute with coconut nectar or any other liquid sweetener.

In a food processor, combine the walnuts, pistachios, almonds, flour, and salt. Pulse until the nuts are finely ground (be careful not to overprocess). Add the raisins and pulse until well-incorporated and the mixture is crumbly. Add the dates, 2 to 3 at a time, pulsing between additions until each date is well-incorporated and the mixture is sticky. (At this point you can add some water, 2 teaspoons at a time, if needed to help it stick together.) Press the mixture firmly and evenly into an 8-inch square baking pan (lined with plastic wrap for easy removal, if desired).

With a pastry brush or a large spoon, spread the agave nectar evenly across the top of the blondies. Place the pan in the freezer to chill for at least 2 hours before cutting and serving.

Store the blondies in an airtight container in the refrigerator for up to 5 days or in the freezer for up to 3 weeks.

## SUBSTITUTIONS

Walnuts, pistachios, almonds: any combination of the three totaling 2 1/2 cups

## VARIATIONS

- Lower-Fat Baklava Blondies: Replace 1/2 to 3/4 cup of the nuts (any kind) with old-fashioned rolled oats.
- Lower-Sugar Baklava Blondies: Omit the agave glaze on top.
- Exotic Baklava Blondies: Pulse a few drops of rosewater into the mixture when you add the raisins.

# Goji Berry Granola Bars

*The maple syrup and tahini in these bars help keep them moist and chewy, and almost make them feel more like a candy bar than a granola bar. That said, they're probably the most nutritious "candy bar" you'll ever eat, considering they're packed with vitamin C from the berries, calcium from the tahini, protein from the nuts and seeds, and a host of other vitamins and minerals.*

1 cup old-fashioned rolled oats
1/2 cup dry almonds
1/2 cup dry sunflower seeds
1 tablespoon ground flaxseed
1/8 teaspoon sea salt
1/2 cup maple syrup
6 tablespoons tahini
1/2 cup goji berries, soaked in very warm water for 20 minutes and drained

YIELD: 12 BARS

**Per bar:** 181 calories, 10g fat (1g sat), 20g carbs, 2g fiber, 5g protein

- *Baking Option*
- *Grain-Free Variation*
- *Nut-Free Variation*
- *Oil-Free*

In a food processor, combine the oats, almonds, sunflower seeds, flax, and salt. Pulse just until the nuts are coarsely chopped. Be very careful not to overprocess here; the nuts should remain rather chunky and the oats should look only slightly chopped.

In a medium bowl, combine the maple syrup and tahini and stir vigorously to combine. Add the dry mixture from the food processor to the maple-tahini wet mixture and stir with a wooden spoon or sturdy spatula until the mixture is sticky and uniformly combined. (If the spoon or spatula isn't cutting it, don't be afraid to use your hands here!) Lastly, squeeze any excess moisture out of the drained goji berries and stir them into the batter. Press the mixture firmly and evenly into an 8-inch square baking pan (lined with parchment paper for easy removal, if desired).

**Make It Raw:** Dehydrate at 110°F for 6 to 8 hours, until the surface feels dry. Remove from the pan and slice into about 12 pieces. Place the bars on a mesh-lined dehydrator tray and dehydrate for 1 to 2 more hours, if desired. Store in an airtight container in the refrigerator for up to a week or in the freezer for up to a month.

**Make It Baked:** Bake in a preheated 300°F oven for 12 to 15 minutes, until the surface looks dry. Let cool completely before slicing and serving. Store in an airtight container in the refrigerator for up to 2 weeks or in the freezer for up to 2 months.

**Make It Easy:** Freeze the bars for at least 2 hours before slicing and serving. Store in an airtight container in the freezer for up to a month.

Though best served straight from the fridge or freezer, you can keep them at room temperature for a few days if you prefer; just expect a softer, less portable bar.

## SUBSTITUTIONS

- Almonds: hazelnuts, walnuts, or Brazil nuts
- Flax: ground chia seed
- Maple syrup: coconut nectar, agave nectar, or any other liquid sweetener
- Tahini: almond butter (page 33), sunseed butter (page 37), or any other nut/seed butter
- Goji berries: raisins or any other small (or chopped) dried fruit

## VARIATIONS

- Grain-Free Granola Bars: Replace the oats with unsweetened flaked coconut and reduce the tahini to 1/4 cup.
- Nut-Free Granola Bars: Replace the almonds with pumpkin seeds or additional sunflower seeds.

# Marzipan Buckeye Bars

*A thin chocolate shell crowns a buttery candied almond layer in these rich, fudge-like treats. I find almond extract to be extremely strong, so I only put in 1/4 teaspoon, but some of my almond-loving recipe testers liked it with a full 1/2 teaspoon—so it's up to you!*

**Marzipan Layer:**
1 cup almond butter (page 33)
1/4 cup coconut nectar
1/4 to 1/2 teaspoon almond
    extract
Big pinch of sea salt
1/4 cup coconut flour

**Chocolate Glaze:**
1/2 cup melted coconut oil
1/4 cup cacao powder
1/4 cup maple syrup
1/2 teaspoon vanilla extract
Big pinch of sea salt

YIELD: 18 SERVINGS

**Per serving:** 178 calories, 15.1g fat (6g sat), 10.7g carbs, 2g fiber, 2.7g protein

- *20 Minutes or Less*
- *Grain-Free*

**Marzipan Layer:** Combine the almond butter, coconut nectar, almond extract (to taste), and salt in a food processor, and pulse until smooth and combined. Add the coconut flour and pulse until the mixture comes together and starts to ball up. Transfer the ball of dough to a 6- to 8-inch square baking pan (lined with waxed paper for easy removal, if desired) and use a spatula or your fingers to press it down evenly. Place the pan in the freezer while you make the topping.

**Chocolate Glaze:** Combine the oil, cacao powder, maple syrup, vanilla, and salt in a blender. Blend on low speed until smooth, stopping to scrape down the sides if necessary. Alternatively, thoroughly whisk all ingredients together in a medium bowl.

Remove the pan from the freezer and immediately pour the glaze over the marzipan, tilting the pan to spread it around evenly. Freeze for at least 2 hours before slicing and serving.

Store the bars in an airtight container in the freezer for up to 3 weeks. Serve frozen.

**SUBSTITUTIONS**
- Almond butter: cashew butter (page 35)
- Coconut nectar: maple syrup, agave nectar, or any other liquid sweetener
- Coconut flour: plain or vanilla nondairy protein powder
- Maple syrup: coconut nectar, agave nectar, or any other liquid sweetener
- Cacao powder: unsweetened cocoa powder or carob powder

**VARIATION**
- Peanut Butter Buckeye Bars: Peanut butter isn't raw, of course, but you can swap in some natural roasted PB for the almond butter here (omitting the almond extract) for more classic buckeye bars.

# Cherry-Carob Bars

*These perfect-for-snacking energy bars contain malty carob powder, tart dried cherries, and no added sugars. If you are a chocoholic, don't like your desserts too sweet, or simply don't keep carob on hand, don't let that stop you from making these—some testers liked them even better with cacao powder in place of carob!*

1 cup dry hazelnuts
1 cup dry sunflower seeds
1/3 cup carob powder
1/8 teaspoon sea salt
1 cup dried cherries
1 cup soft raisins
2 tablespoons water

YIELD: 12 SERVINGS

**Per serving:** 212 calories, 12.8g fat (1g sat), 26.3g carbs, 4g fiber, 4.8g protein

• *20 Minutes or Less*
• *Grain-Free*
• *Lower-Fat Variation*
• *Oil-Free*
• *No Added Sugars*

In a food processor, combine the hazelnuts, sunflower seeds, carob powder, and salt. Pulse until the nuts are finely ground (be careful not to overprocess). Add the cherries and raisins, 1/2 cup at a time, pulsing between additions until each the mixture is homogenous. Add the water and pulse several more times until the mixture is sticky.

Press the mixture firmly and evenly into an 8-inch square baking pan (lined with plastic wrap for easy removal, if desired). Enjoy immediately or place in the refrigerator to chill for at least 2 hours before cutting and serving.

Store the bars in an airtight container in the refrigerator for up to a week or in the freezer for up to a month.

### SUBSTITUTIONS
- Hazelnuts: almonds or pecans
- Sunflower seeds: walnuts or almonds

### VARIATION
- Lower-Fat Cherry-Carob Bars: Replace 1/2 cup of the sunflower seeds with old-fashioned rolled oats.

# Pecan Chai Spice Bars

*Not only does "pecan chai" sound like "pecan pie," but these bars taste a little like pecan pie—with some Eastern flair added. Brew your chai tea long and strong to ensure that you can taste it in the final product. You can either eat these straight out of the freezer, when they'll be solid enough to eat out-of-hand, or enjoy them from the refrigerator, when the buttery topping will be pleasantly gooey and melty.*

**Crust:**
1 cup dry pecans
1/2 cup coconut flour
Big pinch of sea salt
1/4 cup strong brewed chai tea
2 tablespoons maple syrup

**Filling and Topping:**
1/2 cup cashew butter (page 35)
1/4 cup strong brewed chai tea
3 tablespoons maple syrup
Pinch of sea salt
3/4 cup dry pecans, chopped if desired

YIELD: 16 SERVINGS

**Per serving:** 159 calories, 13g fat (2g sat), 10.6g carbs, 3g fiber, 3g protein

- 20 Minutes or Less
- Grain-Free
- Lower-Fat Variation
- Oil-Free

**Crust:** Combine the pecans, coconut flour, and salt in a food processor and pulse until the nuts are finely ground. Add the chai tea and pulse to combine. Add the maple syrup and pulse until the mixture is combined and crumbly. You can add water, a teaspoon at a time, if needed to achieve the desired consistency. Press the mixture firmly and evenly into an 8-inch square baking pan lined with plastic wrap for easy removal, if desired.

**Filling:** Combine the cashew butter, chai tea, maple syrup, and salt in a medium bowl. Stir vigorously to combine. Pour the filling over the crust and scatter the (whole or chopped) pecans on top. Place the pan in the freezer to chill for at least 2 hours before cutting and serving.

Store the bars in an airtight container in the refrigerator for up to 1 week or in the freezer for up to 1 month.

### SUBSTITUTION
- Maple syrup: coconut nectar, agave nectar, or any other liquid sweetener

### VARIATIONS
- Lower-Fat Pecan Chai Bars: Replace 1/3 cup of the pecans in the crust with old-fashioned rolled oats. Reduce the pecans in the topping to 1/2 cup and chop them finely to help you sprinkle them evenly.
- Tea-Free Pecan Chai Bars: Replace the chai tea in both the crust and filling with water, and add about 1/2 teaspoon powdered chai spice mix (or to taste) to each.

# Matt's Banana-Oat Breakfast Bars

*My husband, Matt, wanted a snack that is tasty, nutritious, grab-and-go, and easy to make. I created these bars with some of his favorite ingredients: oats, bananas, raisins, and chocolate. He grabs one of these from the freezer on his way out the door on busy mornings. I also included protein powder to help him refuel after a.m. workouts.*

2 large ripe bananas, peeled and chopped

1/4 cup pitted dates, soaked in warm water for 15 minutes and drained

1 tablespoon ground flaxseed

2 teaspoons lemon juice

1/8 teaspoon sea salt

1 1/2 cups old-fashioned rolled oats

1/2 cup nondairy protein powder

3/4 cup raisins

1/3 cup cacao nibs, chopped frozen Easy Chocolate Bar (page 166), or nondairy chocolate chips

YIELD: 8 BIG BARS

Per serving: 194 calories, 4.5g fat (2g sat), 35.1g carbs, 5g fiber, 9.6g protein

- Baking Option
- Lower-Fat
- Nut-Free
- Oil-Free
- No Added Sugars

**Chef's Tip:** I like using a vanilla-flavored protein powder in these bars.

Combine the banana, dates, flax, lemon juice, and salt in a high-speed blender or food processor. Blend until combined and smooth. Place the oats and protein powder in a large bowl, add the blended mixture, and stir vigorously to combine. Fold in the raisins and cacao nibs or chocolate pieces. Press the mixture firmly and evenly into an 8-inch square baking pan (lined with parchment paper for easy removal, if desired).

**Make It Raw:** Dehydrate at 110°F for 8 to 10 hours, until the surface feels dry. Remove from the pan and slice into bars. Place the bars on a mesh-lined dehydrator tray and dehydrate for 2 to 4 more hours. Store in an airtight container in the refrigerator for up to a week or in the freezer for up to a month.

**Make It Baked:** Bake in a preheated 325°F oven for 12 to 15 minutes, until the surface looks dry and lightly browned. Let cool *completely* before slicing and serving. Store in an airtight container in the refrigerator for up to 2 weeks or in the freezer for up to 2 months.

**Make It Easy:** Freeze the bars for at least 4 hours or overnight before slicing and serving. Store in an airtight container in the freezer for up to a month.

**SUBSTITUTIONS**
- Flax: ground chia seed
- Raisins: any other small (or chopped) dried fruit

# A Piece of Cake

|||||||||||||||||||||||||||||||||||||||||||||||||||||||||||||||||||||||||||||||||||||||||||||||||

## Cakes, Cupcakes, Cheesecakes, Tortes

Cake is such a celebratory dessert. What would a birthday or wedding or graduation or Tuesday be without an epic cake as the grand finale?

Raw cakes, however, have a completely different texture than tall, airy, easy-to-polish-off-three-pieces-in-one-sitting baked cakes—they are dense, thickly-textured, and oh-so-filling. Think "pudding cake" rather than "angel food cake." A base of puréed apples and fluffy coconut flour – a trick I learned from my friend Natalia (nataliakw.com) – allows you to build impossibly-moist raw cakes of any flavor you can dream up. Get ready for a brand new cake experience!

In this chapter you'll drool over cakes, cupcakes, cheesecakes, and tortes of all shapes and styles, accented with fresh fruit, chocolate, nuts, raw frostings and fillings (see Chapter 9), and more. With the few that require dehydration, I provide directions (as always!) for how to bake them in a conventional oven or even freeze them for a whole new take on cake.

Confetti Birthday Cake (page 90)

# Confetti Birthday Cake

*This spectacular cake is a dense, rich interpretation of a classic birthday cake. The colorful sprinkles are a totally optional inclusion, but they sure are fun!*

**Confetti Sprinkles:**
6 tablespoons unsweetened shredded coconut, divided
2 teaspoons spinach juice
2 teaspoons strawberry or beet juice
2 teaspoons blueberry juice

**Cake:**
1 cup unsweetened apple-sauce (see page 39)
1 cup coconut nectar
2 teaspoons lemon juice
1 teaspoon vanilla extract
1/4 teaspoon sea salt
1 cup cashew flour (page 30)
1 1/4 cups coconut flour

**Frosting:**
1 cup Vanilla-Coconut Crème (page 188)

YIELD: 12 SERVINGS

**Per serving:** 272 calories, 13.7g fat (6g sat), 35.4g carbs, 7g fiber, 5.7g protein

- Baking Option
- Grain-Free
- Nut-Free Variation
- Oil-Free

**Confetti Sprinkles:** Divide the shredded coconut among 3 small bowls or ramekins (2 tablespoons per bowl). Add the spinach juice to one bowl, the strawberry or beet juice to another bowl, and the blueberry juice to the third bowl and stir to coat the coconut shreds. Place the bowls in a dehydrator set to 110°F overnight, or lightly toast the coated coconut shreds in a skillet over medium-low heat for a few minutes to dry them out.

**Cake:** Combine the applesauce, coconut nectar, lemon juice, vanilla, and salt in a stand mixer or food processor. Blend until smooth and combined. Add the cashew flour and blend again until smooth. Add the coconut flour and blend or pulse until well-combined. Finally, blend or pulse in the confetti sprinkles (reserving some to dust atop the finished cake, if desired). The mixture will be very thick and dough-like.

**Make It Raw:** Transfer half the batter to a 5- or 6-inch round springform pan (lined with waxed or parchment paper for easy removal, if desired) and pack it down firmly and evenly. Remove the sides of the pan and carefully invert the cake onto a Teflex-lined tray. Repeat with the second half of the batter. Dehydrate the cake halves at 110°F for 1 to 2 hours, flipping them over halfway through, until they have firmed up slightly and the surfaces feel dry.

**Make It Baked:** Preheat the oven to 250°F. Transfer half the batter to a 5- or 6-inch round springform pan (lined with parchment paper for easy removal, if desired) and pack it down firmly and evenly. Remove the sides of the pan and carefully invert the cake onto a parchment-paper-lined baking sheet. Repeat with the second half of the batter. Bake the cake halves for 12 to 14 minutes, flipping them over halfway through, until they have firmed up slightly and the surfaces feel dry.

**Make It Easy:** Transfer half the batter to a 5- or 6-inch round springform pan (lined with waxed or parchment paper for easy removal) and pack it down firmly and evenly. Remove the sides of the pan and carefully invert the cake onto a waxed-paper-lined baking sheet. Repeat with the second half of the batter. Refrigerate or freeze the cake halves until firm.

**Assemble:** When both halves of the cake have firmed up, place one half on a plate or cake stand and thinly frost the top only with Vanilla-Coconut Crème. Carefully place the other cake half on top and use the rest of the icing to frost the top and sides of the cake. Dust with reserved sprinkles and serve immediately.

Snugly wrap leftover cake in plastic wrap and store in the refrigerator for up to 4 days.

## SUBSTITUTIONS

- Coconut nectar: agave nectar or other liquid sweetener
- Cashew flour: almond flour (page 29) or any other nut flour

## VARIATIONS

- Nut-Free Birthday Cake: Replace the cashew flour with Sunflour (page 31) and thinly frost with plain Coconut Butter (page 36) or top with vanilla non-dairy yogurt.
- Classic Birthday Cake: Omit the confetti sprinkles.

# German Chocolate Cake

*German chocolate may not have anything to do with Germany (it was named after a Mr. Samuel German), but it can't be a coincidence that my family (the Lichtenauers) is a GCC-loving clan. My raw version is naturally sweetened with date syrup (see page 38) and topped with a coconut-pecan frosting that'll rival any you've ever tried.*

### Cake:
1/2 cup unsweetened apple-sauce (see page 39)
3/4 cup Date Syrup (page 38)
1/2 teaspoon vanilla extract
1/2 teaspoon lemon juice
1/8 teaspoon sea salt
1/2 cup cacao powder
1/2 cup almond flour
1/2 cup coconut flour
Stevia to taste (optional)

### Frosting:
3/4 cup Date Syrup (page 38)
1/2 cup dry pecans, chopped
1/2 cup unsweetened shred-ded coconut
1/4 teaspoon lemon juice
1/8 teaspoon sea salt

YIELD: 8 SERVINGS

**Per serving:** 234 calories, 13.5g fat (5g sat), 31.3g carbs, 9g fiber, 5g protein

- *Baking Option*
- *Grain-Free*
- *Oil-Free*
- *No Added Sugars*

**Cake:** In a food processor or stand mixer, combine the applesauce, date syrup, vanilla, lemon juice, and salt. Blend until smooth and combined. Add the cacao powder and blend until smooth. Add the almond flour and blend again until smooth. Add the coconut flour and pulse or blend until well-combined. The mixture will be very thick and dough-like. Taste the batter, and if you think it needs a little more sweetness, pulse in stevia to taste.

**Make It Raw:** Press the batter firmly and evenly into a 5- or 6-inch round springform pan (lined with waxed or parchment paper for easy removal, if desired). Remove the sides of the pan and carefully invert the cake onto a Teflex-lined tray. Dehydrate at 115°F for 1 hour (for a moist, pudding-cake-like texture) or 2 hours (for a drier crumb), flipping over halfway through, until the cake has firmed up slightly and the surface feels dry.

**Make It Baked:** Preheat the oven to 250°F. Press the batter firmly and evenly into a 5- or 6-inch round springform pan (lined with parchment paper for easy removal, if desired). Remove the sides of the pan and carefully invert the cake onto a parchment-paper-lined baking sheet. Bake for 10 to 12 minutes, flipping over halfway through, until the cake has firmed up slightly and the surface feels dry.

**Make It Easy:** Press the batter firmly and evenly into a 5- or 6-inch round springform pan (lined with waxed or parchment paper for easy removal, if desired). Refrigerate or freeze the cake until firm.

**Frosting:** To make the coconut-pecan frosting, place all frosting ingredients in a medium bowl and stir together until combined. Alternatively, pulse all frosting ingredients together in a food processor.

When the cake is ready, top it with an even layer of the frosting. Serve immediately or refrigerate until ready to serve. If refrigerated, remove the cake from the fridge about 15 minutes before serving.

Snugly wrap leftover cake in plastic wrap and store in the refrigerator for up to 4 days.

**SUBSTITUTIONS**

- Date Syrup: 1/2 cup maple syrup, coconut nectar, agave nectar, or any other liquid sweetener plus 1/4 cup water
- Cacao powder: unsweetened cocoa powder or carob powder
- Almond flour: cashew flour (page 30) or any other nut flour
- Pecans: walnuts

**VARIATION**

- Chocolate Birthday Cake: Omit the coconut-pecan frost-ing and top the cake with Fluffy Chocolate Frosting (page 189) instead.

# Enlightened Carrot Cake

*Who in their right mind would attempt to create a raw, vegan, gluten-free, grain-free, nut-free, low-calorie, low-fat, no-added-sugar, and no-bake – but still tasty – carrot cake? Well, me. It took some tinkering, but I think you'll love what I came up with. I recommend using a very sweet variety of red apple and the softest, moistest dates you can find. Keep in mind, of course, that this is no longer nut-free when you add the Tangy Cream Cheese Icing, but miraculously, it* is *still low-cal and low-fat!*

1 cup pitted dates, soaked in warm water for 15 minutes and drained

1 large or 2 small red apples, peeled if desired, cored, and chopped

1/4 cup water

1 tablespoon lemon juice

1 teaspoon vanilla extract

1 teaspoon ground cinnamon

1/2 teaspoon ground nutmeg (optional)

1/4 teaspoon sea salt

1 pound carrots, peeled if desired, shredded

3/4 cup coconut flour

Stevia to taste (optional)

1 batch Tangy Cream Cheese Icing (page 190), for frosting

**YIELD:** 8 SERVINGS

**Per serving** (without icing): 147 calories, 1.4g fat (1g sat), 35.7g carbs, 9g fiber, 2.6g protein

**Per serving** (with icing): 241 calories, 7.4g fat (2g sat), 43.9g carbs, 9.5g fiber, 5.2g protein

Combine the drained dates, apple, water, lemon juice, and vanilla in a food processor. Blend until fairly smooth. It may remain just slightly chunky. Add the cinnamon, nutmeg, and salt and blend again until combined.

Place the shredded carrots in a large bowl. Add the mixture from the food processor and stir well with a wooden spoon to combine. Add the coconut flour (if it's clumpy, sift it in). Stir until the batter is combined and uniform. Taste the batter, and if you think it needs a little more sweetness, add stevia to taste. Set the batter aside for 5 to 10 minutes to allow the coconut flour to absorb the liquid mixture.

Divide the batter between two 5- or 6-inch round spring-form pans, pressing it in firmly and evenly, and freeze for 4 hours or refrigerate overnight. (If you only have one pan, you can press half the batter into the pan and freeze it for 2 to 4 hours, placing the bowl with the rest of the batter in the fridge. When the half in the pan has firmed up, remove it to a plate and place it in the fridge. Press the remaining half of the batter into the same pan and freeze for 4 hours or refrigerate overnight.)

When both halves of the cake have firmed up, place one half on a plate or cake stand and frost the top only with Tangy Cream Cheese Icing. Carefully place the other cake half on top, and use the rest of the icing to frost the top and sides of the cake. Refrigerate overnight, or until ready to serve.

Snugly wrap leftover cake in plastic wrap and store in the refrigerator for up to 4 days.

- Grain-Free
- Lower-Fat
- Nut-Free Variation
- Oil-Free
- No Added Sugars

**Chef's Tips:** To make easy work of all those carrots, shred them in a food processor fitted with the grating disc. To make a larger cake in an 8- to 9-inch springform pan, simply double the recipe. This cake tastes best after overnight (or longer!) refrigeration, and will keep well in the fridge for several days.

## SUBSTITUTIONS

- Apple: pear
- Water: coconut water or nondairy milk of choice

## VARIATIONS

- Nut-Free Carrot Cake: Top the cake with your favorite vanilla non-dairy yogurt or a thin layer of coconut butter (page 36) in place of the Tangy Cream Cheese Icing.
- Nutty Carrot Cake: Mix 1/2 cup chopped dry walnuts into the batter.
- Polka-Dot Carrot Cake: Mix 1/2 cup soaked raisins into the batter.

# Maple Streusel Coffee Cake Squares

*These are one of Matt's all-time favorites. Considering the fact that it doesn't contain any chocolate (which he loves), that's really saying something!*

1 cup dry walnuts
1 cup dry pecans
1/2 cup old-fashioned rolled oats
1/4 teaspoon ground cinnamon
1/8 teaspoon sea salt
1/4 cup coconut flour
1/2 cup pitted dates
1 teaspoon vanilla extract
1/4 cup + 1 tablespoon maple syrup, divided
1 tablespoon coconut palm sugar

YIELD: 12 SERVINGS

**Per serving**: 195 calories, 13.6g fat (1g sat), 18.8g carbs, 3g fiber, 3.3g protein

- 20 Minutes or Less
- Grain-Free Variation
- Lower-Fat Variation
- Oil-Free

**Chef's Tip:** If you have mesquite powder on hand, add 2 teaspoons to the batter along with the coconut flour for a delightful flavor enhancement.

- Tropical Carrot Cake: Mix 1/2 cup unsweetened shredded or flaked coconut into the batter.

In a food processor, combine the walnuts and pecans and pulse a few times, until the nuts are roughly chopped. Add the oats, cinnamon, and salt, and pulse just until the nuts are coarsely ground (be careful not to overprocess). Transfer 2/3 cup of the nut mixture to a small bowl and set aside.

Add the coconut flour to the remaining mixture in the food processor and pulse until just combined. Add the dates, 2 to 3 at a time, pulsing between additions until each date is well-incorporated. Add the vanilla and 1/4 cup of the maple syrup and pulse until the mixture clumps together. Transfer the batter to an 8-inch square baking pan (lined with plastic wrap for easy removal, if desired), using your fingers or a spatula to press it firmly and evenly into the pan.

Add the coconut palm sugar and remaining tablespoon of maple syrup to the reserved nut-oat mixture in the small bowl. Use a fork to stir it together until it becomes sticky. Scatter the streusel evenly on top of the cake in the pan, and firmly press it down with your fingers or the bottom of a cup. Refrigerate until ready to cut and serve.

Store the squares in an airtight container in the refrigerator for up to a week or in the freezer for up to a month.

### SUBSTITUTIONS
- Walnuts: additional pecans, or almonds
- Pecans: additional walnuts, or almonds
- Dates: soft golden raisins
- Coconut palm sugar: Sucanat, maple sugar, or organic brown sugar

### VARIATIONS
- Grain-Free Coffee Cake Bars: Replace the oats with unsweetened flaked coconut.
- Lower-Fat Coffee Cake Bars: Replace 1/2 cup of either the pecans or the walnuts with additional old-fashioned rolled oats.

# Pineapple Upside-Down Cake

*My raw pineapple upside-down cake puts the syrupy-sweet classic of the 1970s to shame. This healthier version tastes like pure indulgence.*

**Topping:**
- 2 tablespoons coconut palm sugar
- 1 cup fresh or thawed frozen pineapple chunks, roughly chopped, juice reserved

**Cake:**
- 1/3 cup coconut nectar
- 1/4 cup unsweetened applesauce (see page 39)
- 3 tablespoons reserved pineapple juice
- 2 tablespoons coconut butter (page 36)
- 2 teaspoons lemon juice
- 1/8 teaspoon sea salt
- 3/4 cup cashew flour
- 1/2 cup coconut flour

YIELD: 8 SERVINGS

**Per serving**: 182 calories, 9.1g fat (4g sat), 24.4g carbs, 4g fiber, 3.8g protein

- *Baking Option*
- *Grain-Free*
- *Lower-Fat*
- *Nut-Free Variation*
- *Oil-Free*

**Chef's Tips:** To make the cake in an 8- to 9-inch springform pan, double the recipe. This cake tastes best after overnight refrigeration. It keeps well in the fridge for several days.

**Topping:** Sprinkle the sugar into a 5- or 6-inch round springform pan (lined with parchment paper for easy removal, if desired). Top evenly with the chopped pineapple and set the pan aside.

**Cake:** In a food processor or stand mixer, combine the coconut nectar, applesauce, reserved pineapple juice, coconut butter, lemon juice, and salt. Blend until smooth and combined. Add the cashew flour and blend again until smooth. Finally, add the coconut flour and pulse or blend until well-combined. The mixture will be very thick and dough-like. Carefully transfer the batter into the pan on top of the pineapple, pressing it down firmly and evenly.

**Make It Raw:** Dehydrate at 110°F for 4 to 5 hours, until the cake has firmed up slightly and the top feels dry.

**Make It Baked:** Bake in a preheated 250°F oven for 16 to 20 minutes, until the cake has firmed up slightly and the top feels dry.

**Make It Easy:** Refrigerate or freeze the cake until firm.

**Assemble:** Carefully invert the cake onto a plate or serving platter and remove the sides of the pan. Serve immediately or refrigerate until ready to serve. If refrigerated, remove the cake from the fridge about 15 minutes before serving.

Snugly wrap leftover cake in plastic wrap and store in the refrigerator for up to 3 days.

## SUBSTITUTIONS
- Coconut palm sugar: Sucanat or organic brown sugar
- Coconut nectar: agave nectar or any other liquid sweetener
- Cashew flour: almond flour (page 29) or any other nut flour

## VARIATION
- Nut-Free Pineapple Upside-Down Cake: Replace the cashew flour with Sunflour (page 31).

# Austrian Sacher Torte

*The Sacher Torte is the signature dessert of Vienna, Austria, consisting of two layers of dense, somewhat dry chocolate sponge cake with a thin layer of apricot jam in the middle. The whole cake is coated in dark chocolate ganache icing, and is meant to be enjoyed with a good cup of coffee—though it'll also pair fabulously with a glass of your favorite nondairy milk (see pages 25-28).*

### Cake:
1/2 cup dry walnuts
1/2 cup maple syrup
1/4 cup unsweetened apple-
    sauce (see page 39)
1/4 cup brewed coffee
1 teaspoon vanilla extract
1/2 teaspoon lemon juice
1/8 teaspoon sea salt
1/2 cup cacao powder
3/4 cup coconut flour

### Filling and Ganache:
1/2 batch Fruity Chia Jam
    (page 196), dried fruit ver-
    sion, made with apricots
1/2 batch Sugar-Free Choco-
    late Ganache (page 194)

YIELD: 8 SERVINGS

**Per serving**: 279 calories, 17.6g fat (11g sat), 33.9g carbs, 9g fiber, 4.5g protein

- *Baking Option*
- *Grain-Free*
- *Lower-Fat Variation*
- *Oil-Free Variation*

**Chef's Tip:** To make a larger cake in an 8- to 9-inch spring-form pan, double the recipe.

**Cake:** Place the walnuts in a food processor and pulse until the nuts are finely ground (be careful not to overprocess). Transfer the ground nuts to a small bowl and set aside.

In the same food processor (no need to wash it in between), combine the maple syrup, applesauce, coffee, vanilla, lemon juice, and salt, and blend until smooth and combined. Add the cacao powder and blend until smooth. Add the ground walnuts and blend again until smooth. Finally, add the coconut flour and pulse until well-combined. The mixture will be very thick, slightly crumbly, and dough-like.

**Make It Raw:** Transfer half the batter to a 5- or 6-inch round springform pan (lined with waxed or parchment paper for easy removal, if desired) and pack it down firmly and evenly. Remove the sides of the pan and carefully invert the cake onto a Teflex-lined dehydrator tray. Repeat with the second half of the batter. Dehydrate the cake halves at 110°F for about 2 hours, flipping them over halfway through, until they have firmed up slightly and the surfaces feel dry.

**Make It Baked:** Preheat the oven to 250°F. Transfer half the batter to a 5- or 6-inch round springform pan (lined with parchment paper for easy removal, if desired) and pack it down firmly and evenly. Remove the sides of the pan and carefully invert the cake onto a parchment-paper-lined baking sheet. Repeat with the second half of the batter. Bake the cake halves for 14 to 15 minutes, flipping them over halfway through, until they have firmed up slightly and the surfaces feel dry.

**Make It Easy:** Transfer half the batter to a 5- or 6-inch round springform pan (lined with waxed or parchment paper for easy removal, if desired) and pack it down firmly and evenly. Remove the sides of the pan and carefully invert the cake onto a waxed-paper-lined baking sheet. Repeat with the second half of the batter. Refrigerate or freeze the cake halves until firm.

**Assemble:** When the cake halves are ready, place one half on a wire rack and evenly spread the apricot jam across the top. Carefully place the other half on top. Set the wire rack over a large piece of waxed paper and pour the Sugar-Free Chocolate Ganache on top, spreading it around slightly with a spoon and letting it drizzle down the sides. Let the cake sit at room temperature for 1 to 2 hours, until the ganache has dried slightly and no longer looks glossy. Carefully transfer the cake to a large plate or cake stand. Refrigerate overnight, or until ready to serve.

Snugly wrap leftover cake in plastic wrap and store in the refrigerator for up to 4 days.

## SUBSTITUTIONS
- Walnuts: pecans
- Maple syrup: coconut nectar, agave nectar, or any other liquid sweetener
- Coffee: water or nondairy milk of choice (see pages 25-28)
- Cacao powder: unsweetened cocoa powder or carob powder
- Fruity Chia Jam: 1/2 cup storebought apricot jam or preserves

## VARIATIONS
- Lower-Fat Sacher Torte: Replace the Sugar-Free Chocolate Ganache (page 194) with Fat-Free Chocolate Syrup (page 195).
- Oil-Free Sacher Torte: Replace the Sugar-Free Chocolate Ganache with Fat-Free Chocolate Syrup.
- Nontraditional Sacher Torte: Replace the apricot jam with your favorite fruit jam or preserves.

# Crumb-Topped Chocolate Hazelnut Torte

*This decadent torte features a tender crust and smooth, mild chocolate filling. Chewy oats and crunchy cacao nibs lend terrific texture to the crumb topping.*

**Crust and Topping:**
1/2 cup dry hazelnuts
1/3 cup old-fashioned rolled oats
1/8 teaspoon sea salt
2/3 cup pitted dates
1 tablespoon cacao nibs

**Filling:**
1/2 cup almond butter (page 33)
1/4 cup coconut butter (page 36)
1/4 cup coconut nectar
2 tablespoons cacao powder
2 tablespoons water or non-dairy milk of choice (see pages 25-28)
1/2 teaspoon vanilla extract
1/2 teaspoon hazelnut extract
Pinch of sea salt

YIELD: 8 SERVINGS

**Per serving**: 291 calories, 20.1g fat (6g sat), 26.9g carbs, 4.5g fiber, 5.1g protein

• *Grain-Free Variation*
• *Oil-Free*
• *Lower-Fat Variation*
• *Lower-Sugar Variation*

**Crust and Topping:** In a food processor, combine the hazelnuts, oats, and salt, and pulse until finely ground. Add the dates and pulse until evenly incorporated. The mixture should be crumbly but sticky and homogenous. In a small bowl, combine 1/3 cup of the crust mixture with the cacao nibs; set aside. Press the remainder of the crust mixture firmly and evenly into a 5- or 6-inch round springform pan and place in the freezer to chill while you make the filling.

**Filling:** In a medium bowl, combine all filling ingredients. With a sturdy whisk or wooden spoon, mix until well-combined (it will be very thick). If the mixture is too difficult to stir, add additional water or milk 1 tablespoon at a time until you can stir it smoothly. (Alternatively, you can pulse the filling ingredients together in a mini food processor.)

Remove the pan from the freezer and transfer the chocolate filling onto the crust, spreading it evenly with a spoon or spatula. Crumble the reserved crust-cacao nib mixture on top of the chocolate layer and use a spoon or your fingers to gently press it slightly into the filling. Refrigerate the torte for at least 2 hours before cutting and serving.

Snugly wrap leftover torte in plastic wrap and store in the refrigerator for up to 4 days.

## SUBSTITUTIONS
- Hazelnuts: almonds or almond flour (page 29)
- Dates: raisins or dried cherries
- Coconut nectar: maple syrup, agave nectar, or any other liquid sweetener
- Hazelnut extract: additional vanilla extract

## VARIATIONS
- Grain-Free Chocolate Hazelnut Torte: Replace the oats with unsweetened shredded coconut.
- Lower-Sugar Chocolate Hazelnut Torte: Replace the co-

**Chef's Tips:** For a deeper chocolate flavor, increase the cacao powder in the filling by 1 or 2 tablespoons. To make a larger torte in an 8- to 9-inch springform pan, simply double the recipe.

conut nectar in the filling with 6 tablespoons Date Syrup (page 38).

- Lower-Fat Chocolate Hazelnut Torte: Replace the coconut butter in the filling with plain or vanilla nondairy yogurt and omit the water or milk.
- Crumb-Topped Mocha Torte: Replace the hazelnut extract in the filling with coffee extract and the water or nondairy milk with brewed coffee or espresso.

# New York Cheesecake

*Every raw pastry chef ought to have a winning cheesecake recipe in her portfolio. I sweetened my cheesecakes with agave nectar for years before finally experimenting with stevia, but once I created this version, I knew I'd have no further need for syrupy sweeteners in my cheesecakes.*

**Crust:**
3/4 cup dry almonds
1/8 teaspoon sea salt
1/2 cup pitted dates

**Filling:**
2 cups cashews or macadamia nuts, soaked for 2 to 4 hours and drained
6 tablespoons warm water
1/4 cup melted coconut oil
2 tablespoons lemon juice
1/2 teaspoon vanilla extract
Big pinch of sea salt
1/8 teaspoon pure stevia powder (or equivalent sweetener of choice; see page 12), or to taste

YIELD: 12 SERVINGS

**Per serving**: 273 calories, 21.5g fat (7g sat), 17.5g carbs, 2g fiber, 7g protein

- *Grain-Free*
- *Lower-Fat Variation*
- *Oil-Free Variation*
- *No Added Sugars*

**Crust:** Combine the almonds and salt in a food processor and pulse until the nuts are finely ground. Add the dates, 2 to 3 at a time, pulsing between additions until each date is well-incorporated and the mixture is crumbly but slightly sticky. Transfer the mixture to a 5- or 6-inch round springform pan (lined with waxed or parchment paper for easy removal, if desired). Press the mixture thinly, firmly, and evenly onto the bottom of the pan. Place the pan in the refrigerator while you make the filling.

**Filling:** Combine all ingredients in a high-speed blender and blend until completely smooth. Add additional water (or lemon juice, if you prefer your cheesecake quite tart), 1 tablespoon at a time, as needed to help it blend. Taste for sweetness and add additional stevia as desired.

**Assemble:** Remove the crust from the fridge and pour the filling into it. Tap the pan on the counter several times to coax out any air bubbles. Chill the cheesecake in the freezer for at least 4 hours or in the refrigerator overnight, until the filling has set. Serve cold, straight from the fridge.

Snugly wrap leftover cheesecake in plastic wrap and store in the refrigerator for up to 4 days.

## SUBSTITUTIONS
- Almonds: walnuts or pecans
- Dates: soft raisins

## VARIATIONS
- Oil-Free Cheesecake: Replace the coconut oil with coconut butter (page 36).
- Lower-Fat Cheesecake: Replace 1/4 cup of the almonds in the crust with old-fashioned rolled oats or oat flour (page 32). Replace 1/3 cup of the cashews or macadamia nuts in the filling with plain or vanilla nondairy yogurt and reduce the water to 1/4 cup.
- Stevia-Free Cheesecake: If you're sensititve to the taste of stevia, replace the stevia powder with 1/4 cup of your fa-

vorite liquid sweetener. Taste the mixture for sweetness after blending, and add more sweetener as desired.

- Raspberry Swirl Cheesecake: After pouring the filling onto the crust, drizzle a few spoonfuls of Raspberry Coulis (page 192) on top and swirl together with the tip of a knife.
- Chocolate Cheesecake: Blend 1/3 cup cacao powder (or to taste) into the filling, plus additional sweetener if/as desired.
- Vanilla Bean Cheesecake: Replace the vanilla extract in the filling with the seeds of one vanilla bean.
- Protein Cheesecake: Blend two scoops of your favorite non-dairy protein powder into the filling, adjusting the amounts of water and stevia as needed.

# Lemon Love Cupcakes

*These bright and tangy cupcakes will lend a little extra sunshine to your day. I like to crown each cake with a disc of buttery, melt-in-your-mouth Coconut Lemon Curd, but the Vanilla-Coconut Crème on page 188 also makes a stellar topping.*

1 cup unsweetened apple-
    sauce (see page 39)
3/4 cup coconut nectar
1/4 cup lemon juice
2 tablespoons water
2 teaspoons lemon zest
1/4 teaspoon sea salt
1 cup cashew flour (page 30)
1 cup coconut flour
1 batch Coconut Lemon Curd
    (page 193), for topping

YIELD: 8 LARGE OR 20 MINI
CUPCAKES

**Per large cupcake** (without topping): 246 calories, 9.3g fat (2g
sat), 39g carbs, 7g fiber, 5.3g
protein

**Per mini cupcake** (without topping): 98 calories, 3.7g fat (1g
sat), 15.6g carbs, 3g fiber, 2.1g
protein

- *20 Minutes or Less*
- *Grain-Free*
- *Lower-Fat*
- *Nut-Free Variation*
- *Oil-Free*

Combine the applesauce, coconut nectar, lemon juice, water, lemon zest, and salt in a food processor or stand mixer and blend until smooth and combined. Add the cashew flour and blend again until smooth. Finally, add the coconut flour and pulse or blend until well-combined. The mixture will be very thick and dough-like.

Divide the dough between 8 large or 20 mini muffin cups (with or without paper liners), pressing firmly and evenly into each. Refrigerate until ready to serve. Just before serving, top each cupcake with a spoonful of Coconut Lemon Curd.

Store the cupcakes in an airtight container in the refrigerator for up to 4 days or in the freezer for up to 3 weeks.

## SUBSTITUTIONS
- Coconut nectar: agave nectar, maple syrup, or any other liquid sweetener
- Cashew flour: almond flour (page 29) or any other nut flour
- Coconut Lemon Curd: Vanilla-Coconut Crème (page 188)

## VARIATIONS
- Nut-Free Lemon Cupcakes: Replace the cashew flour with Sunflour (page 31).
- Lime Love Cupcakes: Replace the lemon juice and zest with lime juice and zest.

# Devil's Food Cupcakes

*These soft, moist, and devilishly delicious cupcakes will make any chocolate lover swoon.*

1 cup unsweetened apple-
   sauce (see page 39)
3/4 cup maple syrup
1 1/2 teaspoons vanilla extract
1/2 teaspoon lemon juice
1/4 teaspoon sea salt
3/4 cup cacao powder
1 cup almond flour (page 29)
1 cup coconut flour
1 batch Fluffy Chocolate
   Frosting (page 189), for
   topping

YIELD: 8 LARGE OR 20 MINI
CUPCAKES

**Per large cupcake** (without
frosting): 240 calories, 9.7g fat
(2g sat), 40.5g carbs, 11g fiber,
6.5g protein

**Per mini cupcake** (without
frosting): 107 calories, 4.3g fat
(1g sat), 18g carbs, 5g fiber, 3g
protein

• *20 Minutes or Less*
• *Grain-Free*
• *Lower-Fat*
• *Nut-Free Variation*
• *Oil-Free*

In a food processor or stand mixer, combine the apple-sauce, maple syrup, vanilla, lemon juice, and salt. Blend until smooth and combined. Add the cacao powder and blend until smooth. Add the almond flour and blend again until smooth. Finally, add the coconut flour and pulse or blend until well-combined. The mixture will be very thick and dough-like.

Divide the dough between 8 large or 20 mini muffin cups (with or without paper liners), pressing firmly and evenly into each. Refrigerate until ready to serve. Just before serving, top each cupcake with a dollop or swirl of Fluffy Chocolate Frosting.

Store leftover unfrosted cupcakes in an airtight container in the refrigerator for up to 4 days or in the freezer for up to 3 weeks.

## SUBSTITUTIONS

- Maple syrup: coconut nectar, agave nectar, or any other liquid sweetener
- Cacao powder: unsweetened cocoa powder or carob powder
- Almond flour: cashew flour (page 30) or any other nut flour
- Fluffy Chocolate Frosting: Sugar-Free Chocolate Ganache (page 194)

## VARIATIONS

- Nut-Free Devil's Food Cupcakes: Replace the almond flour with Sunflour (page 31).
- Comida del Diablo Cupcakes: Add 1 teaspoon ground cinnamon and 1/8 teaspoon cayenne pepper along with the cacao powder.
- German Chocolate Cupcakes: Top the cupcakes with the coconut-pecan frosting from the German Chocolate Cake recipe on page 92 instead of the Fluffy Chocolate Frosting.
- Pick-Your-Poison Devil's Food Cupcakes: Replace the vanilla extract with 1/2 teaspoon of another flavor extract, such as coffee, hazelnut, almond, or peppermint.

# Strawberry Shortcupcakes

*Tender, biscuit-like cake layers snuggle sweet strawberries under a river of rich cashew cream in these seductive, summery treats.*

1/2 cup unsweetened apple-sauce (see page 39)
1/4 cup coconut nectar
2 tablespoons coconut butter (page 36)
1 teaspoon lemon juice
1/2 teaspoon vanilla extract
1/8 teaspoon sea salt
1/2 cup cashew flour (page 30)
6 tablespoons coconut flour
1/2 batch Vanilla-Coconut Crème (page 188)
1/2 cup hulled, sliced fresh strawberries

YIELD: 8 SHORTCUPCAKES

**Per shortcupcake:** 199 calories, 12.8g fat (6g sat), 19.6g carbs, 4g fiber, 4.5g protein

- *Grain-Free*
- *Nut-Free Variation*
- *Lower-Fat Variation*
- *Oil-Free*

**Chef's Tip:** A mini food pro-cessor works best for this, but you could double the recipe and make it in a regular (11- to 14-cup) food processor. Trust me, you won't have any prob-lem finishing off the bigger batch!

Combine the applesauce, coconut nectar, coconut butter, lemon juice, vanilla, and salt in a food processor. Blend un-til smooth and combined. Add the cashew flour and blend again until smooth. Finally, add the coconut flour and pulse until well-combined. The mixture will be very thick and dough-like.

Divide the dough between 16 mini muffin cups (with paper liners, if you have them), filling them only about halfway full and pressing the dough firmly and evenly into each. Refrigerate for 4 hours or freeze for 1 hour, or until ready to serve.

Just before serving, place 8 of the cupcakes right-side-up on a plate. Top each with a heaping 1/2 tablespoon of the Vanilla-Coconut Crème. Arrange a few strawberry slices on top, then top with the remaining 8 cupcakes, placing them upside-down on the strawberries. Dollop another heaping 1/2 tablespoon of the Vanilla-Coconut Crème onto each, and arrange a few more strawberry slices on top if desired. Serve with a fork!

Store leftover unfilled cupcakes in an airtight container in the refrigerator for up to 4 days or in the freezer for up to 3 weeks.

### SUBSTITUTIONS
- Coconut nectar: agave nectar or any other liquid sweetener
- Cashew flour: almond flour (page 29) or any other nut flour

### VARIATION
- Lower-Fat Shortcupcakes: Top the cakes with your fa-vorite vanilla non-dairy yogurt, instead of the Vanilla-Coconut Crème.
- Nut-Free Shortcupcakes: Replace the cashew flour with Sunflour (page 31) and use plain coconut butter (page 36) or vanilla non-dairy yogurt in place of the Vanilla-Coconut Crème.

# Coconut Heaven Cupcakes

*Buckle your seatbelts, coconut lovers—these cupcakes will catapult you straight into the stratosphere of coconut heaven.*

1 cup unsweetened apple-
    sauce (see page 39)
1/2 cup coconut nectar
1/4 cup coconut butter (page
    36), plus more for topping
1/4 cup water
2 teaspoons coconut extract
1 teaspoon lemon juice
1/4 teaspoon sea salt
1 cup cashew flour (page 30)
1 cup coconut flour
Unsweetened shredded or
    flaked coconut, for topping
    (optional)

YIELD: 8 LARGE OR 20 MINI
CUPCAKES

**Per large cupcake** (without topping): 233 calories, 12.2g fat (6g sat), 29.9g carbs, 8g fiber, 5g protein

**Per mini cupcake** (without topping): 93 calories, 4.9g fat (2g sat), 12g carbs, 3g fiber, 2g protein

- *20 Minutes or Less*
- *Grain-Free*
- *Lower-Fat Variation*
- *Nut-Free Variation*
- *Oil-Free*

Combine the applesauce, coconut nectar, coconut butter, water, coconut extract, lemon juice, and salt in a food processor. Blend until smooth and combined. Add the cashew flour and blend again until smooth. Add the coconut flour and pulse until well-combined. The mixture will be very thick and dough-like.

Divide the dough between 8 large or 20 mini muffin cups (with or without paper liners), pressing firmly and evenly into each. Refrigerate until ready to serve. Just before serving, top each cupcake with a spoonful of softened coconut butter and sprinkle with shredded or flaked coconut.

Store leftover unfrosted cupcakes in an airtight container in the refrigerator for up to 4 days or in the freezer for up to 3 weeks.

## SUBSTITUTIONS
- Coconut nectar: agave nectar or any other liquid sweetener
- Cashew flour: almond flour (page 29) or any other nut flour
- Coconut butter: Vanilla-Coconut Crème (page 188)

## VARIATIONS
- Lower-Fat Coconut Cupcakes: Reduce the coconut butter to 2 tablespoons. Replace 1/3 cup of the cashew flour with oat flour (page 32). Top with plain nondairy yogurt (again, coconut yogurt would be best) instead of coconut butter, or simply leave unfrosted.
- Nut-Free Coconut Cupcakes: Replace the cashew flour with Sunflour (page 31).

**Chef's Tip:** If you don't have coconut extract, feel free to leave it out or replace it with 1 teaspoon vanilla extract (the coconut flavor will then, of course, be less pronounced). True coconut freaks can even mix 1/4 cup shredded coconut into the dough.

# Almond Butter Banana Cupcakes

*Nut butter and banana is a classic pairing in my book, and these filling (yet oil-free and no added sugars) cupcakes can double as a satisfying dessert or a healthy breakfast.*

2 medium ripe bananas, peeled and chopped

1/2 cup pitted dates, soaked in warm water for 15 minutes and drained

1/4 cup almond butter (page 33)

2 tablespoons water or non-dairy milk of choice (pages 25-28)

2 teaspoons lemon juice

1 teaspoon vanilla extract

1/8 teaspoon sea salt

1/4 cup almond flour (page 29)

3/4 cup coconut flour

Sliced bananas and additional almond butter (page 33), for topping

YIELD: 7 LARGE OR 18 MINI CUPCAKES

**Per large cupcake** (without topping): 190 calories, 8.8g fat (2g sat), 28.6g carbs, 8g fiber, 4.5g protein

**Per mini cupcake** (without topping): 74 calories, 3.4g fat (1g sat), 11.1g carbs, 3g fiber, 1.7g protein

- 20 Minutes or Less
- Grain-Free
- Lower-Fat
- Nut-Free Variation
- Oil-Free
- No Added Sugars

Combine the bananas, drained dates, almond butter, water, lemon juice, vanilla, and salt in a food processor and blend until smooth and combined. Add the almond flour and blend again until smooth. Finally, add the coconut flour and pulse until well-combined. The mixture will be very thick and dough-like.

Divide the dough between 7 large or 18 mini muffin cups (with or without paper liners), pressing firmly and evenly into each. Refrigerate until ready to serve. Just before serving, top each cupcake with a spoonful of almond butter and a few banana slices.

Store leftover unfrosted cupcakes in an airtight container in the refrigerator for up to 4 days or in the freezer for up to 3 weeks.

## SUBSTITUTIONS
- Almond butter: cashew butter (page 35) or any other nut butter
- Almond flour: cashew flour (page 30) or any other nut flour

## VARIATIONS
- Nut-Free Banana Cupcakes: Replace the almond butter with sunseed butter (page 37) and the almond flour with Sunflour (page 31).
- Peanut Butter Banana Cupcakes: Replace the almond butter with natural peanut butter.

# Square Root of Pie

||||||||||||||||||||||||||||||||||||||||||||||||||||||||||||||||||||||||||||||||||||||||||||||||||

## Pies, Tarts, Cobblers, Crisps

**P**ies are comfort food at its finest. Who doesn't have memories of enjoying freshly baked pie alongside family at the holidays, or à la mode in the summer? Tarts are equally versatile—whether covered in chocolate or decorated with fresh fruit, a tart is an elegantly impressive end to any meal.

Raw pies and tarts are so easy to make and delectable to devour that I can't even remember the last time I baked one. They can be bright and fruity, chilly and refreshing, dark and decadent, cool and creamy, or anything else you want them to be, all without turning on an oven. Raw tarts and pies are also my favorite way to showcase juicy, colorful, seasonal fruit. Nuts, seeds, and dried fruits create perfect crusts every time – no wrestling with unruly and temperamental pie dough – and the possibilities for fresh, luscious fillings and toppings are limitless.

In this chapter you'll find pies and tarts (or tartlets) aplenty, plus a few cobblers, crisps, and tortes. Best of all, they're almost all prepared by simply mixing, layering, and refrigerating!

Summer Fruit Pizza (page 128)

# Deep-Dish Caramel Apple Pie

*Picture it: a tender, nutty crust and crumble topping, surrounding caramel-coated apple slices kissed with cinnamon, all gently warmed in the dehydrator or oven. In other words, autumnal heaven. That is this pie.*

**Crust and Topping:**
1 1/2 cups dry almonds
3/4 cup dry walnuts
3/4 cup dry pecans
1/8 teaspoon sea salt
3/4 cup soft golden raisins
1/3 cup pitted dates

**Filling:**
3 medium red apples, peeled, cored, and thinly sliced
1 tablespoon lemon juice
3/4 teaspoon ground cinnamon (or to taste)
1 batch Ooey Gooey Caramel Sauce (page 191)

YIELD: 12 SERVINGS

**Per serving:** 283 calories, 16.1g fat (1g sat), 35.1g carbs, 6g fiber, 5.2g protein

- *Baking Option*
- *Grain-Free*
- *Lower-Fat Variation*
- *Oil-Free*
- *No Added Sugars*

**Crust:** Combine the almonds, walnuts, pecans, and salt in a food processor and pulse until the nuts are finely ground. Add the raisins, 1/4 cup at a time, pulsing between additions until well-incorporated. Add the dates and pulse until the mixture is sticky but still crumbly. Measure out 1 cup of this crust mixture and set it aside.

Transfer the remaining crust mixture to a deep-dish 9-inch pie plate (lined with parchment paper for easy removal, if desired). Press the mixture thinly, firmly, and evenly onto the sides and bottom of the pan. Set the pan aside while you make the filling.

**Filling:** Combine the sliced apples with the lemon juice and cinnamon in a large bowl and toss to combine. Add the Ooey Gooey Caramel Sauce and toss again until the apple slices are all coated with the caramel. Transfer the apple mixture (and any extra caramel lingering at the bottom of the bowl) into the reserved crust, arranging the apples and patting them down so they create a flat, even layer. Evenly crumble the reserved 1 cup of the crust mixture on top of the apples.

**Make It Raw:** Dehydrate at 115°F for 5 to 6 hours, until the pie is just barely warm to the touch.

**Make It Baked:** Bake in a preheated 250°F oven for 20 to 25 minutes, until warmed throughout. Let cool slightly before eating.

**Make It Easy:** Refrigerate until ready to serve.

Snugly wrap leftover pie in plastic wrap and store in the refrigerator for up to 3 days.

**SUBSTITUTIONS**
- Almonds: hazelnuts
- Walnuts: additional pecans or Brazil nuts
- Pecans: additional walnuts or macadamia nuts
- Dates: soft raisins

## VARIATIONS

- Lower-Fat Caramel Apple Pie: Replace 1 cup of the almonds in the crust with old-fashioned rolled oats.
- Caramel Pear Pie: Replace the apples with ripe pears.

# Key Lime Pie

*Travel to the Florida Keys without leaving your kitchen with this tart 'n tangy pie. Avocado is the secret ingredient that gives the filling its fluffy-yet-creamy quality.*

### Crust:
3/4 cup dry macadamia nuts
1/2 cup unsweetened shredded coconut
1 teaspoon lime zest (optional)
1/8 teaspoon sea salt
1/2 cup soft golden raisins

### Filling:
1/4 cup coconut butter (page 36)
1/4 cup coconut nectar
1/4 cup lime juice
1 teaspoon lime zest (optional)
Big pinch of sea salt
1 large, ripe avocado, pitted, peeled, and chopped (about 1 cup chopped flesh)

YIELD: 8 SERVINGS (4 MINI TARTLETS)

**Per serving** (1/2 tartlet): 266 calories, 20.5g fat (9g sat), 22g carbs, 5g fiber, 2.6g protein

- *Grain-Free*
- *Lower-Fat Variation*
- *Oil-Free*
- *Lower-Sugar Variation*

**Chef's Tip**: To make a larger pie in 9-inch pie plate, simply double the recipe.

**Crust:** In a food processor, combine the macadamia nuts, coconut, zest, and salt and pulse until the nuts are finely ground. Add the raisins and pulse until the mixture is crumbly but sticky and homogenous. Divide the crust mixture between four 4-inch mini tartlet pans with removable bottoms. Press the mixture firmly and evenly onto the bottoms and sides of the pans and place them in the freezer to chill while you make the filling.

**Filling:** In a food processor or high-speed blender, combine the coconut butter, coconut nectar, lime juice, zest, and salt; process until smooth. Add the avocado and blend until completely smooth and fluffy. Remove the crusts from the freezer and divide the filling among them, tapping the pans on the countertop to help the filling settle. Refrigerate for at least 2 hours before serving.

Snugly wrap leftover pies in plastic wrap and store in the refrigerator for up to 3 days.

### SUBSTITUTIONS
- Macadamia nuts: almonds or almond flour (page 29)
- Golden raisins: pitted dates
- Coconut nectar: agave nectar, maple syrup, or any other liquid sweetener

### VARIATIONS
- Lower-Fat Key Lime Pie: Replace 1/4 cup of the macadamia nuts in the crust with old-fashioned rolled oats. Use a small avocado in the filling (about 3/4 cup chopped flesh) and add 1/4 cup plain or vanilla nondairy yogurt.
- Lower-Sugar Key Lime Pie: Replace the coconut nectar in the filling with 6 tablespoons cup Date Syrup (page 38).
- Key Lime Mousse: Ditch the crust and serve the filling in wine or martini glasses.
- Luscious Lemon Pie: Replace the lime juice and zest with lemon juice and zest.
- Lime-In-The-Coconut Pie: Add 1 teaspoon coconut extract to the filling and top the filled pies with a generous dusting of unsweetened shredded coconut.
- Margarita Pie: Blend a tablespoon of tequila into the filling.

# French Silk Pie

*This classic, triple-layered delight consists of a mixed nut crust, a silken chocolate-avocado pudding filling, and a dreamy cashew cream topping, all made without added sugars.*

**Crust:**
1/2 cup dry almonds
1/2 cup dry pecans
1/2 cup dry cashews
1/8 teaspoon sea salt
3/4 cup pitted dates

**Filling:**
1 large, ripe avocado, pitted, peeled, and chopped (about 1 cup)
3/4 cup nondairy milk of choice (pages 25-28)
1/4 cup pitted dates
1/4 cup cacao powder
2 tablespoons melted coconut oil
1 teaspoon lemon juice
Big pinch of sea salt
20 to 25 drops liquid stevia (or equivalent sweetener of choice; see page 12), or to taste

**Topping:**
3/4 cup cashews, soaked for 2 to 4 hours and drained
1/3 cup + 1 tablespoon nondairy milk of choice (pages 25-28)
1 tablespoon melted coconut oil
1/2 teaspoon lemon juice
Pinch of sea salt
15 to 20 drops liquid stevia (or equivalent sweetener of choice; see page 12), or to taste

**Crust:** Combine the almonds, pecans, cashews, and salt in a food processor and pulse until the nuts are finely ground. Add the dates, 2 to 3 at a time, pulsing between additions until each date is well-incorporated and the mixture is crumbly but slightly sticky. You can add another date or two if needed to achieve the desired texture. Transfer the mixture to a 9-inch pie plate (lined with plastic wrap for easy removal, if desired). Press the mixture thinly, firmly, and evenly onto the sides and bottom of the pan. Place the pan in the refrigerator while you make the chocolate filling.

**Filling:** Combine all ingredients in a high-speed blender or food processor and blend until completely smooth. Taste for sweetness and add more stevia if desired. Remove the crust from the fridge and pour in the chocolate mixture from the blender, spreading it evenly into the crust with a spatula or large spoon. Tap the pan on the counter several times to spread the filling around. Place the pan back in the refrigerator while you make the topping.

**Topping:** Combine all ingredients in a high-speed blender and blend until completely smooth. Taste for sweetness and add more stevia if desired. Remove the pie from the fridge again and pour the cream from the blender over the chocolate layer, carefully spreading it evenly to the edges of the crust with a spatula or large spoon. Chill the pie in the refrigerator for 6 to 8 hours or overnight, until the filling has set. Serve cold. Snugly wrap leftover pie in plastic wrap and store in the refrigerator for up to 3 days.

### SUBSTITUTIONS
- Almonds: additional cashews or pecans
- Pecans: walnuts or Brazil nuts
- Cashews: macadamia nuts
- Dates: soft raisins

### VARIATIONS
- Lower-Fat French Silk Pie: Replace the cashews in the crust with old-fashioned rolled oats. Reduce the coconut oil in the filling to 1 tablespoon. Replace 1/4 cup of the cashews in the topping with plain or vanilla nondairy yogurt and reduce the milk to 1/3 cup.

- *Grain-Free*
- *Lower-Fat Variation*
- *Oil-Free Variation*
- *No Added Sugars*

■ Oil-Free French Silk Pie: Replace the coconut oil in the filling and topping with coconut butter (page 36).

**Chef's Tips:** Divide the crust and filling between six to eight 4-inch tartlet pans to make mini French silk pies. If you're sensitive to the taste of stevia, I suggest replacing it with another sweetener of your choice (see page 12 for guidelines) in this pie.

# Blueberry Dream Pie

*There are no words for how creamy, dreamy, and luscious this pie is. When blended, blueberries become naturally gelatinous, helping the filling set up properly. A cashew cream swirl adds an extra element of fancy.*

**Crust:**
1 cup dry walnuts
1/2 cup dry almonds
1/8 teaspoon sea salt
3/4 cup pitted dates

**Filling:**
1 cup cashews, soaked for 2 to 4 hours and drained
2 tablespoons melted coconut oil
1 tablespoon lemon juice
1/2 teaspoon vanilla extract
Big pinch of sea salt
10 drops liquid stevia (or equivalent sweetener of choice; see page 12), or to taste (optional)
1 (10-ounce) package frozen wild blueberries, thawed

YIELD: 12 SERVINGS

**Per serving**: 219 calories, 16g fat (4g sat), 18.1g carbs, 3g fiber, 4.7g protein

- *Grain-Free*
- *Lower-Fat Variation*
- *Nut-Free Variation*
- *Oil-Free Variation*
- *No Added Sugars*

**Crust:** Combine the walnuts, almonds, and salt in a food processor and pulse until the nuts are finely ground. Add the dates, 2 to 3 at a time, pulsing between additions until each date is well-incorporated and the mixture is crumbly but slightly sticky. Transfer the mixture to a 9-inch pie plate (lined with plastic wrap for easy removal, if desired). Press the mixture thinly, firmly, and evenly onto the sides and bottom of the pan. Place the pan in the refrigerator while you make the filling.

**Filling:** Combine the cashews, coconut oil, lemon juice, vanilla, salt, and stevia (if desired) in a high-speed blender and blend until completely smooth. Transfer about 3/4 cup of the mixture from the blender into a small bowl and set aside. Add the blueberries to the remaining mixture in the blender and blend until very smooth.

Remove the crust from the fridge and pour in the blueberry filling from the blender. Tap the pan on the counter several times to spread the filling around. Drop the reserved cashew cream in large spoonfuls on top of the blueberry filling. With the tip of a knife, make decorative loops across the top of the pie, swirling the cashew and blueberry fillings together (be careful not to over-swirl, though). Chill the pie in the freezer for at least 4 hours or in the refrigerator overnight, until the filling has set. Serve cold.

Snugly wrap leftover pie in plastic wrap and store in the refrigerator for up to 3 days.

**SUBSTITUTIONS**
- Walnuts: pecans
- Almonds: pecans or additional walnuts
- Dates: soft raisins
- Cashews: macadamia nuts

**VARIATIONS**
- Lower-Fat Blueberry Pie: Replace the almonds in the crust with old-fashioned rolled oats. Replace 1/4 cup of the cashews in the filling with plain or vanilla nondairy yogurt or 1/2 medium, very ripe peeled banana.

- Nut-Free Blueberry Pie: In the crust, replace the walnuts with sunflower seeds and the almonds with unsweetened shredded coconut. In the filling, replace the cashews with 1/2 cup coconut butter plus 1/2 cup water or coconut water.
- Oil-Free Blueberry Pie: Replace the coconut oil with coconut butter (page 36).
- Blueberry-Carob Pie: Add 2 tablespoons carob powder to the crust mixture, and 1 tablespoon to the filling too, if desired.
- Blueberry-Banana Pie: Arrange a single layer of thin, ripe banana slices onto the crust before pouring on the blueberry filling.

**Chef's Tip:** Divide the crust and filling between six to eight 4-inch tartlet pans to make mini cream pies. Try using mini chocolate chips or chopped or shaved Easy Chocolate Bar (page 166) as a topping instead of the sliced banana.

# Coco-Nana Cream Pie

*In trying to develop a coconut cream pie without using fresh coconut meat, I employed a touch of coconut flour and a ripe banana, and found the resulting pie to be even yummier than the sum of its parts. Coconut cream and banana cream are two all-star flavors in the world of pies, and it turns out they combine beautifully.*

**Crust:**
1 cup unsweetened shredded coconut
2/3 cup dry almonds
1/8 teaspoon sea salt
1 cup pitted dates

**Filling:**
1 large or 2 small very ripe bananas, peeled
1 cup coconut water
3/4 cup coconut butter (page 36)
1/4 cup coconut nectar
2 tablespoons coconut flour
1 teaspoon lemon juice
Big pinch of sea salt

**Topping:**
Unsweetened flaked coconut
1 medium ripe banana, peeled and sliced

YIELD: 12 SERVINGS

**Per serving**: 253 calories, 16.8g fat (13g sat), 26.4g carbs, 6g fiber, 3.3g protein

- Grain-Free
- Lower-Fat Variation
- Nut-Free Variation
- Oil-Free
- Lower-Sugar Variation

**Crust:** Combine the coconut, almonds, and salt in a food processor and pulse until the nuts are finely ground. Add the dates, 2 to 3 at a time, pulsing between additions until well-incorporated and the mixture is crumbly but slightly sticky. Transfer to a 9-inch pie plate or tart pan with removable bottom. Press the mixture thinly, firmly, and evenly onto the sides and bottom of the pan. Place the pan in the refrigerator while you make the filling.

**Filling:** combine all ingredients in a high-speed blender and blend until *completely* smooth. Remove the crust from the fridge and spread the filling evenly into it. Tap the pan on the counter a few times to coax out any air bubbles. Place back in the refrigerator to chill for at least 4 to 6 hours or overnight, until the filling has set.

Serve chilled, garnished with coconut flakes and sliced bananas, if desired. Snugly wrap leftover pie in plastic wrap and store in the refrigerator for up to 3 days.

## SUBSTITUTIONS
- Almonds: walnuts or cashews
- Dates: soft golden raisins
- Coconut water: plain water plus 2 additional tablespoons coconut nectar
- Coconut nectar: agave nectar or any other liquid sweetener

## VARIATIONS
- Lower-Fat Coco-Nana Pie: Replace 1/2 cup of the shredded coconut in the crust with old-fashioned rolled oats. Replace 1/4 cup of the coconut butter in the filling with plain or vanilla nondairy yogurt and reduce the coconut water to 3/4 cup.
- Nut-Free Coco-Nana Pie: Replace the almonds in the crust with sunflower seeds.
- Lower-Sugar Coco-Nana Pie: Replace the coconut nectar in the filling with 1/3 cup Date Syrup (page 38).
- Classic Coconut Cream Pie: Replace the banana with 1/3 cup macadamia nuts or cashews, soaked for 2 to 4 hours and drained.

# Summer Fruit Pizza

*Dessert pizza rocks. This colorful pie makes use of all manner of fresh summer fruit. Raspberry sauce mimics marinara and crushed macadamia nuts make perfect "cheese" sprinkles. I like to take the illusion even further by cutting my fruit to resemble pepperoni slices, diced green pepper, and other typical savory pizza toppings!*

**Crust:**
1 cup dry pecans
1/2 cup dry cashews
1/8 teaspoon sea salt
1/4 cup golden raisins
1/4 cup pitted dates

**Sauce:**
1/2 batch Raspberry Coulis
    (page 192)

**Cheese Sprinkles:**
1/2 cup dry macadamia nuts or
    cashews
1 teaspoon lemon juice
5 to 10 drops liquid stevia
    (optional)
Pinch of sea salt

**Toppings:**
1 cup fresh strawberries,
    hulled and sliced
1 medium ripe kiwifruit,
    peeled and diced
1/3 cup diced pineapple
    chunks
1/4 cup fresh blueberries
Fresh mint leaves, for garnish
    (optional)

**Yield: 10 servings**

**Per serving:** 214 calories, 16.1g fat (2g sat), 17.4g carbs, 4g fiber, 3.4g protein

**Crust:** Combine the pecans, cashews, and salt in a food processor and pulse until finely ground (be careful not to overprocess). Add the golden raisins and pulse until incorporated. Add the dates and pulse until well-incorporated and the mixture begins to stick together. Transfer the mixture to a 9-inch tart pan with removable bottom. Press the mixture thinly, firmly, and evenly onto the bottom of the pan. Place the pan in the refrigerator or freezer while you prepare the remaining components.

**Cheese Sprinkles:** Combine all ingredients in a food processor (a mini one works well here) and pulse until crumbly.

**Assemble:** Remove the crust from the fridge or freezer and spread the Raspberry Coulis on top, leaving a thin ring of crust open around the edge. Evenly sprinkle the nut "cheese" bits across the sauce, then evenly distribute the toppings on the pizza. Chill in the refrigerator until ready to serve. Snugly wrap leftover "pizza" in plastic wrap and store in the refrigerator for up to 3 days.

## SUBSTITUTIONS
- Pecans: walnuts or almonds
- Cashews: macadamia nuts
- Raspberry Coulis: Fruity Chia Jam (page 196), any variation
- Toppings: any fresh berries or chopped fruit of your choice!

## VARIATIONS
- Lower-Fat Fruit Pizza: Replace 1/2 cup of the pecans in the crust with old-fashioned rolled oats. Omit the cheese sprinkles.
- Chocolate Fruit Pizza: Add 1/4 cup cacao powder to the crust mixture. Replace the Raspberry Coulis with about 1 cup Fat-Free Chocolate Syrup (page 195) or Sugar-Free Chocolate Ganache (page 194).
- Alfredo Fruit Pizza: Replace the Raspberry Coulis with Vanilla-Coconut Crème (page 188) and omit the cheese sprinkles.

- Grain-Free
- Lower-Fat Variation
- Oil-Free
- No Added Sugars

**Chef's Tip:** Divide the crust, sauce, cheese, and toppings between six to eight 4-inch tartlet pans to make mini fruit pizzas.

# Dark Chocolate Truffle Tart with Macaroon Crust

*This tart is part chewy macaroon, part silky truffle, and all chocolate. It's so rich that a small sliver will satisfy even the most dedicated chocoholic.*

**Crust:**
3/4 cup unsweetened shred-
    ded coconut
6 tablespoons almond flour
    (page 29)
3 tablespoons cacao powder
1/8 teaspoon sea salt
2/3 cup pitted dates

**Filling:**
6 tablespoons melted coco-
    nut oil
1/4 cup melted cacao butter
1/4 cup coconut nectar
1 teaspoon vanilla extract
1/8 teaspoon sea salt
1/4 cup cacao powder
2 tablespoons water

YIELD: 12 TO 16 SERVINGS

**Per serving:**(if 12). 207 calories, 16.9g fat (12g sat), 15.3g carbs, 3g fiber, 1.7g protein

**Per serving:**(if 16). 155 calories, 12.7g fat (9g sat), 11.5g carbs, 2g fiber, 1.3g protein

• *Grain-Free*
• *Lower-Fat Variation*
• *Nut-Free Variation*
• *Lower-Sugar Variation*

**Crust:** In a food processor, combine the coconut, almond flour, cacao powder, and salt. Pulse until combined. Add the dates and pulse until well-incorporated. The mixture should be crumbly but sticky and homogenous. Press the mixture firmly and evenly into a 9-inch tart pan with a removable bottom and place in the refrigerator to chill while you make the filling.

**Filling:** In a high-speed blender, combine the coconut oil, cacao butter, coconut nectar, vanilla, and salt. Blend until smooth. Add the cacao powder and blend on low speed until incorporated. Leave the blender on and slowly stream in the water; blend until smooth. (Alternatively, you may whisk all ingredients together in a medium bowl.)

Remove the pan from the refrigerator and transfer the chocolate filling onto the crust, spreading it thinly and evenly with a spoon or spatula. You may want to very gently tap the pan on the counter a few times to coax out any air bubbles. Refrigerate the tart for at least 2 hours before cutting and serving.

Snugly wrap leftover tart in plastic wrap and store in the refrigerator for up to 4 days.

**SUBSTITUTIONS**
- Almond flour: cashew flour (page 30) or oat flour (page 32)
- Cacao powder: unsweetened cocoa powder or carob powder
- Dates: soft raisins
- Cacao butter: additional coconut oil
- Coconut nectar: maple syrup, agave nectar, or any other liquid sweetener

**VARIATIONS**
- Lower-Fat Chocolate Tart: Replace the almond flour in the crust with oat flour (page 32). Replace 2 tablespoons of the coconut oil in the filling with plain or vanilla non-dairy yogurt.

**Chef's Tips:** Add a lovely pop of color by garnishing the plate (or the tart itself) with a drizzle of Raspberry Coulis (page 192). To make a smaller tart in a 5- or 6-inch spring-form pan, simply halve the recipe.

- Nut-Free Chocolate Tart: Replace the almond flour in the crust with Sunflour (page 31).
- Lower-Sugar Chocolate Tart: Replace the coconut nectar in the filling with 6 tablespoons Date Syrup (page 38).
- Nutella Truffle Tart: Replace 1/2 teaspoon of the vanilla extract in the filling with 1 teaspoon hazelnut extract. Optionally, also replace the almond flour in the crust with ground hazelnuts.
- Dark Chocolate Mocha Tart: Replace 1/2 teaspoon of the vanilla extract in the filling with 1 teaspoon coffee extract and/or 1 teaspoon instant coffee granules.
- Chocolate Cherry Truffle Tart: Replace the dates in the crust with dried cherries.

**Chef's Tips:** No need to buy a can of pineapple juice for 1 tablespoon; instead, reserve the juice from the chopped pineapple you use to top the tarts. For easy mixing, bring all filling ingredients to room temperature before combining. To make a larger tart in a 9-inch tart pan, simply double the recipe.

# Tropical Fruit Tartlets

*You might even call these "trawpical." (Yes, it's ok to laugh at me.)* **Note:** Mix the filling and slice the toppings just before serving.

**Crust:**
1 cup dry macadamia nuts
1/2 cup unsweetened shredded coconut
1 teaspoon lime zest or juice (optional)
1/8 teaspoon sea salt
1/2 cup soft golden raisins

**Filling:**
1/4 cup coconut butter (page 36)
1 tablespoon coconut water
1 tablespoon pineapple juice

**Topping:**
2 small ripe kiwifruit, peeled and sliced
1 small ripe banana, peeled and sliced
1/2 small ripe mango, peeled, seeded, and sliced
6 tablespoons diced fresh pineapple
Squeeze of lime juice (optional)

YIELD: 8 SERVINGS (4 MINI TARTLETS)

**Per serving:** (1/2 tartlet). 274 calories, 21.2g fat (9g sat), 22.8g carbs, 6g fiber, 3g protein

• Grain-Free
• Lower-Fat Variation
• Nut-Free Variation
• Oil-Free
• No Added Sugars

**Crust:** Combine the macadamia nuts, coconut, zest (if using), and salt in a food processor. Pulse until the nuts are finely ground. Add the raisins and pulse until the mixture is crumbly but sticky and homogenous. Divide the crust mixture between four 4-inch mini tartlet pans with removable bottoms. Press the mixture firmly and evenly onto the bottoms and sides of the pans. Chill them in the refrigerator for at least 4 hours or in the freezer for at least 2 hours, until ready to assemble and serve.

**Filling:** Combine the coconut butter, coconut water, and pineapple juice in a small bowl. Stir vigorously to combine.

Remove the crusts from the freezer and divide the filling among them, about 1 heaping tablespoon per tartlet, spreading it evenly in the tart shells. Each tart will only get a thin layer of the filling, but that's ok, because the fruit is the star here. Top with the assorted fresh sliced fruit and a squeeze of lime juice, if desired, and serve immediately.

Snugly wrap leftover tartlets in plastic wrap and store in the refrigerator for up to 2 days.

## SUBSTITUTIONS
- Macadamia nuts: cashews, almonds, or 1 scant cup cashew or almond flour
- Golden raisins: pitted dates
- Coconut water: water, nondairy milk of choice (pages 25-28), or additional pineapple juice
- Fruit toppings: any combination of colorful sweet fruit you like. Papaya, cantaloupe, or honeydew melon would make delicious swaps or additions.

## VARIATION
- Lower-Fat Tropical Tartlets: Replace 1/2 cup of the macadamia nuts in the crust with old-fashioned rolled oats. Replace the filling with plain or vanilla nondairy yogurt (preferably coconut yogurt!).
- Nut-Free Tropical Tartlets: Replace the macadamia nuts in the crust with sunflower seeds.

# Linzer Torte

*Named after Linz, Austria, the Linzer torte is a traditional Northern European pastry often enjoyed at Christmastime. This may be my favorite recipe in this entire book—and that's saying something. It's astonishing how so few ingredients can create such a drop-dead-delicious (yet healthy) treat. The lattice-style top crust takes a little extra time and effort, but it sure looks impressive.*

**Crust:**
1 1/4 cups dry hazelnuts
1 cup dry pecans
1/8 teaspoon sea salt
1 heaping cup pitted dates
1/4 cup coconut flour
2 to 6 tablespoons water

**Filling:**
1/2 batch Fruity Chia Jam (page 196), fresh fruit version, made with raspberries

YIELD: 10 SERVINGS

**Per serving:** 283 calories, 19.5g fat (2g sat), 28.3g carbs, 7g fiber, 4.8g protein

- *Grain-Free*
- *Oil-Free*
- *No Added Sugars*

**Chef's Tips:** Divide the crusts and filling between six to eight 4-inch tartlet pans to make mini Linzer tortes. If the crust strips start to fall apart as you braid them, that's ok—I can tell you this torte will taste just as good no matter what it looks like!

**Crust:** Combine the hazelnuts, pecans, and salt in a food processor. Pulse until the nuts are finely ground. Do not overprocess. Add the dates, 2 to 3 at a time, pulsing between additions until well-incorporated and the mixture is sticky. Transfer all but 1 cup of the mixture to a 9-inch tart pan with removable bottom. Press the mixture thinly, firmly, and evenly onto the bottom of the pan, then place in the refrigerator.

To the remaining 1 cup crust mixture in the food processor, add the coconut flour and pulse to combine. Turn on the machine and stream in the water, 1 tablespoon at a time, processing until the mixture starts to ball up (use only as much water as you need to get it sticky and homogenous). Transfer the dough onto a large square of waxed paper (or a silicone mat or Teflex sheet) on a work surface and press it firmly into a 9-inch round. You can place another sheet of waxed paper on top and use a rolling pin to flatten it out if you want. Carefully transfer the flattened dough (still on the waxed paper) to the freezer for at least 1 hour. While it's chilling, prepare the raspberry chia jam.

**Assemble:** Remove the pan with the bottom crust from the fridge and spread the jam thinly and evenly on top, going almost all the way to the edges. Remove the rolled-out top crust from the freezer and slice into thin strips. Carefully arrange and/or braid the strips on top of the jam in a cross-hatch or lattice style. Refrigerate for at least 1 hour, or until ready to serve. Snugly wrap leftover torte in plastic wrap and store in the refrigerator for up to 3 days.

### SUBSTITUTIONS
- Hazelnuts: walnuts or almonds
- Pecans: walnuts or almonds
- Dates: soft raisins
- Fruity Chia Jam: Raspberry Coulis (page 192)

**Chef's Tip:** Instead of making four mini cherry crumbles, you can make one big batch, layering every-thing in a small pan (a 9x5-inch loaf pan works well here) instead of individual ramekins.

# Individual Cherry Crumbles

*These cheery cherry delights are like miniature cherry pies you eat with a spoon. Naturally sweetened with dates, you can add stevia as you please, depending on whether you prefer your cherries tart or sweet. I like the malty, mysterious flavor the carob powder lends, but feel free to leave it out, or even replace with cacao or cocoa powder.*

**Filling:**
1/2 cup pitted dates, soaked in warm water for 15 minutes and drained
1 tablespoon lemon juice
1 tablespoon carob powder (optional)
Big pinch of sea salt
1 pound fresh or thawed frozen pitted sweet cherries, divided
Stevia to taste (optional)

**Topping:**
1/3 cup dry pecans
1/4 cup unsweetened shredded coconut
Big pinch of sea salt
1/3 cup pitted dates

YIELD: 4 SERVINGS

**Per serving**: 288 calories, 10.4g fat (4g sat), 51g carbs, 8g fiber, 3.3g protein

- *20 Minutes or Less*
- *Grain-Free*
- *Lower-Fat Variation*
- *Nut-Free Variation*
- *Oil-Free*
- *No Added Sugars*

**Filling:** Combine the drained dates, lemon juice, carob, salt, and 4 ounces (1/4 pound) of the pitted cherries in a food processor. Blend into a rough purée. Add the remaining 12 ounces (3/4 pound) of the cherries and pulse until the just-added cherries are chopped but still chunky. Taste for sweetness, and pulse in some stevia if desired. Divide the mixture among four 4-ounce (1/2 cup) or slightly larger ramekins, mason jars, or decorative glasses.

**Topping:** Combine the pecans, coconut, and salt in the same food processor (no need to wash it in between) and pulse until the pecans are coarsely chopped. Add the dates and pulse until they're well-incorporated and the mixture is sticky. Spoon the crumbles on top of the cherry filling in each ramekin/glass, dividing the topping evenly among them. Serve immediately, refrigerate until ready to serve, or serve warm. (To serve the crumbles warm, simply warm in a dehydrator at 115°F for about an hour before serving OR in a 200°F oven for about 20 minutes.)

Snugly wrap leftover crumbles in plastic wrap and store in the refrigerator for up to 3 days.

**SUBSTITUTIONS**
- Dates: soft raisins
- Carob powder: cacao powder or unsweetened cocoa powder
- Pecans: walnuts or almonds

**VARIATIONS**
- Lower-Fat Cherry Crumbles: Replace the coconut shreds in the topping with old-fashioned rolled oats.
- Nut-Free Cherry Crumbles: Replace the pecans with sunflower seeds or pumpkin seeds.
- Cherry-Almond Crumbles or Cherry-Vanilla Crumbles: Add 1/2 teaspoon almond extract or 1 teaspoon vanilla extract to the filling mixture.

# Strawberries & Crème Tart

*Doesn't this tart just scream "summer!"? Make sure to buy the sweetest, juiciest, ripest organic strawberries you can find—since this tart has no added sugars, the strawberries take center stage.*

**Crust:**
1 cup dry cashews
1/2 cup dry macadamia nuts
1/8 teaspoon sea salt
3/4 cup pitted dates

**Filling:**
1 batch Vanilla-Coconut
   Crème (page 188)

**Topping:**
12 ounces fresh strawberries,
   hulled and sliced
2 teaspoons lemon juice

YIELD: 12 SERVINGS

**Per serving**: 244 calories, 17.7g fat (5g sat), 20.1g carbs, 3.5g fiber, 5.5g protein

• *Grain-Free*
• *Lower-Fat Variation*
• *Oil-Free*
• *No Added Sugars*

**Chef's Tip**: Divide the crust, filling, and strawberries between six to eight 4-inch tartlet pans to make mini strawberry tarts.

Combine the cashews, macadamia nuts, and salt in a food processor. Pulse until the nuts are finely ground. Add the dates, 2 to 3 at a time, pulsing between additions until each date is well-incorporated and the mixture is crumbly but slightly sticky. Transfer the mixture to a 9-inch tart pan with removable bottom. Press the mixture thinly, firmly, and evenly onto the sides and bottom of the pan. Place the pan in the refrigerator while you make the filling.

When the filling is ready, remove the crust from the fridge and spread the Vanilla-Coconut Crème evenly into it. Return to the refrigerator to chill for 2 hours, or until the filling has set.

Toss the sliced strawberries with the lemon juice, then remove the filled crust from the fridge and decoratively arrange the berries on the tart. Serve immediately or refrigerate until ready to serve. Snugly wrap leftover tart in plastic wrap and store in the refrigerator for up to 3 days.

## SUBSTITUTIONS
- Cashews: additional macadamia nuts
- Macadamia nuts: cashews, pecans, or walnuts
- Dates: soft golden raisins
- Vanilla-Coconut Crème: plain coconut butter (page 36), if you don't have as much of a sweet tooth

## VARIATIONS
- Lower-Fat Strawberry Tart: Reduce the cashews in the crust to 1/2 cup and add 1/3 cup old-fashioned rolled oats. Replace the Vanilla-Coconut Crème with vanilla nondairy yogurt.
- Chocolate Strawberry Tart: Replace the Vanilla-Coconut Crème with about 1 cup Fat-Free Chocolate Syrup (page 195) or Sugar-Free Chocolate Ganache (page 194).
- Strawberry-Banana Tart: Arrange a single layer of thin, ripe banana slices onto the crust before pouring on the crème filling.
- Red White & Blue Tart: Scatter fresh blueberries onto the tart after arranging the strawberries.
- Fruit & Crème Tart: Replace strawberries with any other cut fresh fruit you like.

# Vanilla Bean Peach Cobbler

*Filled with sweet, juicy peaches and a hint of vanilla, this cobbler is pure comfort-food goodness.*

**Crust:**
1 cup dry pecans
1/4 cup coconut flour
1/4 cup coconut palm sugar
1/8 teaspoon sea salt
1/4 cup pitted dates
1/4 cup water

**Filling:**
4 cups sliced fresh ripe
   peaches or thawed frozen
   peaches, divided
1/4 cup cashews, soaked for
   2 to 4 hours and drained
Seeds from 1/2 vanilla bean
10 to 15 drops liquid stevia
   (or equivalent sweetener of
   choice; see page 12), or to
   taste (optional)

YIELD: 8 SERVINGS

**Per serving:** 185 calories, 12.3g fat (2g sat), 19.2g carbs, 4g fiber, 3g protein

- *Baking Option*
- *Grain-Free*
- *Lower-Fat Variation*
- *Oil-Free*
- *Lower-Sugar Variation*

**Chef's Tip:** Divide the crust and filling between six to eight 1/2 to 1 cup ramekins to make mini peach cobblers.

**Crust:** Combine the pecans, coconut flour, sugar, and salt in a food processor. Pulse until the nuts are finely ground (be careful not to overprocess). Add the dates and pulse until well-incorporated. Add the water and pulse until the mixture begins to stick together but is still crumbly. Transfer the mixture onto a large square of waxed paper (or a silicone mat or Teflex sheet) on a countertop or cutting board and pat it firmly into a rough 9-inch square about 1/4 inch thick. You can place another sheet of waxed paper on top and use a rolling pin to flatten it out if you want. Carefully transfer the flattened dough (still on the waxed paper) to the freezer for at least 1 hour.

**Filling:** Combine 1 cup of the peach slices with the cashews and vanilla bean in a high-speed blender and blend until smooth. Taste for sweetness, and if the peaches didn't make it sweet enough, add stevia to taste. Place the remaining 3 cups of peaches in a 9-inch square baking pan (lightly greased with coconut oil, if desired). Pour the mixture from the blender over the peaches and stir them around to coat them.

Remove the flattened crust from the freezer and carefully invert it onto the peach mixture in the pan. It may break apart a little; that's ok. (Just call it "rustic"!)

**Make It Raw:** Dehydrate at 115°F for 3 to 4 hours, until the center is just slightly warm to the touch.

**Make It Baked:** Bake in a preheated 250°F oven for 15 to 17 minutes, until the crust barely begins to brown. Let cool slightly before eating.

**Make It Easy:** Serve immediately, or refrigerate until ready to serve.

Though best served immediately, you may store leftover cobbler in a covered container in the refrigerator for up to 2 days.

## SUBSTITUTIONS

- Pecans: walnuts
- Coconut palm sugar: Sucanat, date sugar, or organic brown sugar
- Cashews: macadamia nuts
- Vanilla bean: 1 1/2 teaspoons vanilla extract

## VARIATIONS

- Lower-Fat Peach Cobbler: Replace 1/3 cup of the pecans with old-fashioned rolled oats. Replace the cashews with plain or vanilla nondairy yogurt.
- Lower-Sugar Peach Cobbler: Omit the coconut palm sugar in the crust and increase the dates to 1/2 cup.
- Blackberry-Peach Cobbler: Omit the vanilla and stir 1 cup fresh blackberries into the peach mixture.
- Peach Melba Cobbler: Omit the vanilla and drizzle Raspberry Coulis (page 192) over individual portions of the cobbler just before serving.

# The Proof Is in the Pudding

## Ice Creams, Puddings, Mousses

**P**udding cups in lunchboxes...ice cream on a sweltering hot summer day...sneaking leftover chocolate mousse for breakfast...I think it's safe to say we all have a soft spot in our hearts for spoonable sweets. Far too often, though, the kind you find in stores (or even restaurants) contain more additives, preservatives, artificial colors and flavors, and emulsifiers than actual food. Raw food to the rescue!

Raw puddings may not have the arrestingly neon coloring of the kinds that come in boxes (which is a good thing!), but they're infinitely more delicious and nutritious. No whipped cream is required to make a fluffy raw mousse, and you can enjoy raw ice cream, sorbet, and gelato all without the use of dairy, refined sugar, or anything fake.

This chapter is filled with a variety of recipes that have one important trait in common: they're enjoyed with a spoon. Puddings, mousses, and ice creams and other frozen treats all get their moment to shine here. Just blend, chill, and enjoy!

Gelato di Avocado (page 163)

# Easy Chia Pudding

*It doesn't get any easier than this, folks. Chia pudding may look a little funny, but it tastes all kinds of delicious and has a delightful tapioca-like texture. I often eat this for breakfast with some berries or chopped fruit.*

1 1/2 cups nondairy milk of choice (pages 25-28)
1/4 cup chia seeds
Pinch of sea salt
Liquid stevia to taste (or sweetener of choice; see page 12)

YIELD: 2 SERVINGS

**Per serving** (made with almond milk): 189 calories, 10.9g fat (1g sat), 19.5g carbs, 12g fiber, 5.5g protein

*Nutritional values may vary depending on your choice of nondairy milk.

• 20 Minutes or Less
• Grain-Free
• Nut-Free
• Oil-Free
• No Added Sugars

**Chef's Tip:** If your nondairy milk is at room temperature when you mix it with the chia seeds, the pudding will only need about 30 minutes to thicken up.

Stir the milk, chia seeds, and salt together in a medium bowl or container. Set aside for 2 to 4 hours, or refrigerate overnight, to allow the mixture to gel and thicken up. Stir again, sweeten with stevia to taste, top with whatever you like (see Variations below), and enjoy.

Store leftover pudding in an airtight container in the refrigerator for up to 2 days.

## VARIATIONS

- Vanilla Chia Pudding: Stir in 1 teaspoon vanilla extract when you combine the seeds and milk.
- Chocolate Chia Pudding: Whisk in 2 tablespoons cacao powder and 1/4 teaspoon vanilla extract when you combine the seeds and milk.
- Berrylicious Chia Pudding: Just before eating, top each serving with 1/4 to 1/2 cup fresh berries (any kind, or a mixture).
- Crunchy Chia Pudding: Just before eating, top each serving with 1 to 2 tablespoons mixed seeds or chopped nuts.
- Protein Chia Pudding: Whisk in 1 scoop nondairy protein powder when you combine the seeds and milk, plus a couple extra tablespoons of milk or water, if needed.

# Velvety Chocolate Mousse

*For some of you, avocado pudding is probably old news, but for others of you, this might be the beginning of a beautiful friendship. Avocado creates a silken texture that you have to taste to believe (and I promise you won't notice any avocado flavor).*

2 large, ripe avocados, pitted, peeled, and chopped (about 2 cups chopped flesh)
1/3 cup water or nondairy milk of choice (see pages 25-28)
1/2 teaspoon vanilla extract
Big pinch of sea salt
2/3 cup pitted dates, soaked in very warm water for 15 minutes and drained
1/3 cup cacao powder
Stevia to taste (optional)

YIELD: 4 SERVINGS

**Per serving**: 260 calories, 16.2g fat (3g sat), 33.5g carbs, 9g fiber, 3.8g protein

- *20 Minutes or Less*
- *Grain-Free*
- *Lower-Fat Variation*
- *Nut-Free*
- *Oil-Free*
- *No Added Sugars*

Combine the avocados, water, vanilla, and salt in a high-speed blender or a food processor. If you don't have a high-speed blender, use the food processor here, not a conventional blender. Blend until smooth and combined, using the tamper if necessary with the high-speed blender.

Add the dates and blend again until well-combined and smooth. You will need to use the tamper here with the blender. Add the cacao powder, put on the lid (so you don't get dusted in chocolate!), and blend again until smooth. Taste for sweetness and add stevia, if desired. Serve immediately.

Store leftover mousse in an airtight container in the refrigerator for up to 1 day.

## SUBSTITUTIONS
- Dates: 1/3 cup maple syrup or coconut nectar (reducing or omitting the water)
- Cacao powder: unsweetened cocoa powder or carob powder

## VARIATIONS
- Lower-Fat Chocolate Mousse: Use only 1 1/2 avocados (about 1 1/2 cups chopped flesh), add 1/3 cup plain or vanilla nondairy yogurt, and reduce the water or milk to 1/4 cup.
- Mexican Chocolate Mousse: Add 1/4 to 1/2 teaspoon ground cinnamon and a pinch of cayenne pepper.
- Mocha Mousse: Use strong brewed coffee or espresso in place of the water or nondairy milk and add 1/4 teaspoon coffee extract, if desired.

**Chef's Tips:** I do not recommend halving this recipe unless you have a mini food processor you can use, otherwise it will be very difficult to blend smoothly. For an even fluffier texture, blend in 1 to 2 teaspoons sunflower lecithin.

# Not-Your-Grandma's Banana Pudding

*I absolutely adore the Just-Like-Grandma's Banana Pudding in* Practically Raw, *but I wanted to create a lighter version. This one has fewer calories, less fat, and less sugar than the original. Since there are no artificial preservatives or food colorings here, the pudding will darken as it chills. Slice some fresh ripe bananas on top to brighten it up.*

2 medium, very ripe bananas, peeled and chopped
1/3 cup cashews, soaked for 2 to 4 hours and drained
2 tablespoons water
1 tablespoon coconut butter (page 36)
2 teaspoons lemon juice
1/2 teaspoon vanilla extract
1/8 teaspoon sea salt
10 to 20 drops liquid stevia (or equivalent sweetener of choice; see page 12), or to taste

YIELD: 4 SERVINGS

**Per serving**: 173 calories, 7.7g fat (3g sat), 25g carbs, 2g fiber, 3g protein

• Grain-Free
• Lower-Fat
• Nut-Free Variation
• Oil-Free
• No Added Sugars

Combine all ingredients in a high-speed blender and blend until smooth. Taste for sweetness and texture, and add a little more water or stevia if needed. Transfer the mixture to a bowl or container and refrigerate for at least 1 to 2 hours before serving (pudding will thicken as it chills). To prevent a skin from forming on the surface of the pudding, refrigerate with a piece of plastic wrap pressed directly on the surface, if desired.

Store the pudding in an airtight container in the refrigerator for up to 2 days.

## SUBSTITUTIONS
- Cashews: macadamia nuts
- Coconut butter: melted coconut oil

## VARIATIONS
- Nut-Free Banana Pudding: Omit the cashews and increase the coconut butter to 1/4 cup.
- Even-Lower-Fat Banana Pudding: Reduce the cashews to 3 tablespoons, add 3 tablespoons plain or vanilla non-dairy yogurt, and reduce the water to 1 tablespoon.

**Chef's Tip:** My recipe tester Kayti discovered that squeezing some fresh lemon juice on top of the pudding before storing it in the refrigerator helped preserve the pudding's banana-yellow color!

# Protein Power Pudding

*This nutritious pudding can be eaten as dessert or a post-workout treat. See Resources (page 199) for information on what brands of protein powder I recommend.*

3/4 cup nondairy milk of choice (pages 25-28)

1/2 cup water

2 scoops (about 40 grams) vanilla-flavored nondairy protein powder

2 tablespoons coconut butter (page 36)

Pinch of sea salt

Stevia to taste (or other sweetener of choice; see page 12), if needed

YIELD: 2 TO 3 SERVINGS

**Per serving** (if 2): 194 calories, 11.1g fat (8g sat), 10g carbs, 4.5g fiber, 17.5g protein

**Per serving** (if 3): 130 calories, 7.4g fat (5g sat), 6.7g carbs, 3g fiber, 11.6g protein

*Nutritional values will vary slightly depending on the brand of protein powder used.

• 20 Minutes or Less
• Grain-Free
• Nut-Free
• Oil-Free
• No Added Sugars

Combine the water, milk, protein powder, coconut butter, and salt in a high-speed blender. Blend until smooth. Taste for sweetness and add stevia or another sweetener, if desired. Transfer the mixture to a bowl or container and refrigerate for at least 1 to 2 hours before serving. The pudding will thicken as it chills.

Store the pudding in an airtight container in the refrigerator for up to 2 days.

### SUBSTITUTION
■ Coconut butter: melted coconut oil

### VARIATION
■ Chocolate Power Pudding: Use chocolate protein powder instead of vanilla, OR blend in 2 tablespoons cacao powder or unsweetened cocoa powder.

# Dulce de Leche Spooncream

*In my first book* Practically Raw, *I explained that "spooncream" is my word for a thin, pudding-like dessert you eat with a spoon. This stuff is very rich, so I keep the serving size fairly small—for a fun presentation, serve it in decorative espresso cups with tiny spoons.*

1 cup cashews, soaked for 2 to 4 hours and drained
3/4 cup coconut milk (page 28) or other nondairy milk of choice (pages 25-28)
1/2 cup pitted dates, soaked in warm water for 20 to 30 minutes and drained
2 tablespoons coconut butter (page 36)
2 teaspoons vanilla extract
1 teaspoon lemon juice
1/8 teaspoon sea salt

YIELD: 6 SERVINGS

**Per serving:** 219 calories, 13.7g fat (5g sat), 21.7g carbs, 3g fiber, 5.2g protein

- *20 minutes or less*
- *Grain-Free*
- *Oil-Free*
- *No Added Sugars*

**Chef's Tip:** A small dollop of Vanilla-Coconut Crème (page 188) makes a nice topping for this spooncream.

Combine all ingredients in a high-speed blender or food processor. Blend until completely smooth. If using a food processor or regular blender, you may need to add water or additional milk, 1 tablespoon at a time, to help it blend smoothly. Refrigerate for 6 to 8 hours or overnight before serving. The spooncream will thicken as it chills.

Store the spooncream in an airtight container in the refrigerator for up to 2 days.

## SUBSTITUTIONS
- Cashews: macadamia nuts
- Coconut butter: melted coconut oil

# Kheer (Indian Rice Pudding)

*My favorite way to end an Indian food feast is with a bowl of sweet rice pudding. Chia seeds replace the grain in this recipe, which can be served chilled or warmed (see the Chef's Tip below).*

1 1/4 cups coconut water
1 cup coconut milk (page 28)
or other nondairy milk of
choice (pages 25-28)
1/2 cup cashews, soaked for
2 to 4 hours and drained
1/4 cup coconut nectar
2 tablespoons coconut butter
(page 36)
2 teaspoons lemon juice
1 teaspoon vanilla extract
1/8 teaspoon ground cinnamon
1/8 teaspoon sea salt
Dash of ground cardamom
(optional)
1/2 cup white chia seeds
1/4 cup golden raisins

YIELD: 8 SERVINGS

Per serving: 199 calories, 11.6g
fat (4g sat), 21.7g carbs, 7g fiber, 4.3g protein

• Grain-Free
• Lower-Fat Variation
• Nut-Free Variation
• Oil-Free

Combine the coconut water and milk, cashews, coconut nectar and butter, lemon juice, vanilla, cinnamon, salt, and cardamom (if desired) in a high-speed blender. Blend until smooth. Transfer the mixture to a bowl or container and whisk in the chia seeds and raisins. Refrigerate for 6 to 8 hours or overnight before serving. The pudding will thicken as it chills.

Store the pudding in an airtight container in the refrigerator for up to 3 days, or freeze for up to 2 weeks, defrosting completely before eating.

## SUBSTITUTIONS
- Coconut water: plain water plus 2 additional tablespoons coconut nectar
- Cashews: macadamia nuts or pistachios
- Coconut nectar: agave nectar or other liquid sweetener
- Coconut butter: melted coconut oil
- White chia seeds: regular (black) chia seeds
- Golden raisins: regular (dark) raisins or chopped dried apricots

## VARIATIONS
- Lower-Fat Kheer: Reduce the coconut water to 1 cup, omit the coconut butter, and blend in a heaping 1/4 cup of plain or vanilla nondairy yogurt.
- Nut-Free Kheer: Replace the cashews with sunflower seeds.
- Protein-Packed Kheer: Blend in a scoop or two of vanilla nondairy protein powder, adding a touch more water or milk if needed.

**Chef's Tip:** If you enjoy your rice pudding warm, you can heat a serving on the stove in a small saucepan over low heat until just warmed throughout.

# Sugar-Free Chocolate Pudding

*This stevia-sweetened, smooth 'n silky pudding is the total package: high in plant-based protein and healthy fats, and free of all sugars (even fruit sugars).*

3/4 cup water or nondairy milk of choice (pages 25-28)

1 large, ripe avocado, pitted, peeled, and chopped (about 1 cup chopped flesh)

1 scoop (about 20 grams) chocolate-flavored non-dairy protein powder

3 tablespoons cacao powder

25 to 35 drops liquid stevia (or equivalent sweetener of choice; see page 12), or to taste

Big pinch of sea salt

**YIELD: 2 SERVINGS**

**Per serving:** 210 calories, 16.4g fat (3g sat), 11.5g carbs, 7g fiber, 10.2g protein

*Nutritional values will vary slightly depending on the brand of protein powder used.

- 20 Minutes or Less
- Grain-Free
- Lower-Fat Variation
- Nut-Free
- Oil-Free
- No Added Sugars

Combine the water or milk, avocado, protein powder, cacao powder, stevia, and salt in a high-speed blender or a food processor. If you don't have a high-speed blender, you'll want to use the food processor here, not a conventional blender. Blend until smooth and combined, using the tamper if necessary with the high-speed blender. Taste for sweetness and add additional stevia to taste, if desired. Serve immediately.

Store leftover pudding in an airtight container in the refrigerator for up to 1 day.

### SUBSTITUTIONS
- Protein powder: 1 additional tablespoon cacao powder
- Cacao powder: unsweetened cocoa powder or carob powder

### VARIATIONS
- Lower-Fat Chocolate Pudding: Use a small avocado (about 3/4 cup chopped flesh) instead of a large one and blend in 1/4 cup plain or vanilla nondairy yogurt.
- Green Chocolate Pudding: Blend in a small handful of spinach leaves.

**Chef's Tips:** For a deeper chocolate flavor, add an additional tablespoon of cacao powder. For a thinner pudding, add 2 more tablespoons water or milk; for a thicker pudding, reduce the water or milk by 2 to 4 tablespoons. For a fluffy, "whipped" texture, blend in 1 to 2 teaspoons sunflower lecithin.

(opposite)

Banana Soft Serve (page 162)

# Create-Your-Own Ice Cream

*When it comes to "lightening up" ice cream, you have a choice: you can cut the sugar or the fat, but not both. This sugar-free ice cream is rich in healthy raw fats, but I do employ a little banana to help cut the fat content somewhat—unless you're very sensitive to the taste of banana, it doesn't seem to noticeably affect the flavor, especially once you start adding mix-ins. The inclusion of vodka is a "grandmother trick" to help the ice cream stay creamy in the freezer (since alcohol never freezes solid), but certainly leave it out if you'd prefer.*

1 1/2 cups cashews or macadamia nuts, soaked for 2 to
  4 hours and drained
1 1/2 cups water or nondairy
  milk of choice (pages 25-28)
2 tablespoons coconut butter
  (page 36) or melted coconut oil
1/4 teaspoon pure stevia
  powder (or 1/2 cup liquid
  sweetener of choice)
1/4 teaspoon sea salt
1 large, very ripe banana,
  peeled
1 tablespoon vodka (optional)

**YIELD:** 6 SERVINGS

**Per serving**: 245 calories, 18.7g
fat (5g sat), 16.4g carbs, 2g fiber, 7g protein

• Grain-Free
• Lower-Fat Variation
• Oil-Free
• No Added Sugars

Combine all ingredients in a high-speed blender and blend until smooth. Taste for sweetness and add additional stevia if desired. Transfer the mixture to an ice cream maker and freeze according to the manufacturer's directions.

# Ice Cream Flavor Options

**Lower-Fat Ice Cream:** If you don't mind a little more banana flavor, reduce the cashews to 1 cup and blend in another ripe banana.

**Vanilla Bean Ice Cream:** Blend in 1 whole vanilla bean or 1 tablespoon vanilla extract.

**Chocolate Ice Cream:** Blend in 1/3 to 1/2 cup cacao powder or unsweetened cocoa powder.

**Mint Chocolate Chip Ice Cream:** Blend in 1 teaspoon peppermint extract and a very large handful of fresh spinach leaves. Add 1/3 cup (or more) cacao nibs or nondairy chocolate chips to the ice cream maker near the end of the freezing time.

**Butter Pecan Ice Cream:** Replace the stevia with 1/2 cup coconut nectar or coconut palm sugar. Add 1/3 cup (or more) chopped dry pecans to the ice cream maker near the end of the freezing time.

**Strawberry Ice Cream:** Reduce the water to 3/4 cup and blend in 2 heaping cups of hulled, halved strawberries. If desired, add 1/2 cup diced strawberries to the ice cream maker near the end of the freezing time.

**Java Chip Ice Cream:** Blend in 4 teaspoons instant coffee powder or 2 teaspoons coffee extract, or use brewed coffee in place of the water. Add 1/3 cup (or more) cacao nibs or nondairy chocolate chips to the ice cream maker near the end of the freezing time.

**Caramel Fudge Ripple Ice Cream:** Slowly pour about 1/3 cup Ooey Gooey Caramel Sauce (page 191) and about 1/3 cup Fat-Free Chocolate Syrup (page 195) into the ice cream maker near the end of the freezing time.

**Brownie Batter Ice Cream:** Add chunks of leftover brownies (such as the Ultimate Raw Brownies on page 67) to the ice cream maker near the end of the freezing time.

**Raspberry Swirl Ice Cream:** Slowly pour 1/2 cup Raspberry Coulis (page 192) or storebought raspberry jam into the ice cream maker near the end of the freezing time.

**Cookie Dough Ice Cream:** Add chunks of leftover cookies (such as the Chocolate Chunk Cookies on page 42) to the ice cream maker near the end of the freezing time.

**Horchata Helado:** Blend in 4 teaspoons vanilla extract and 2 teaspoons ground cinnamon.

**Protein Ice Cream:** Blend in a scoop or two of your favorite nondairy protein powder.

# Mango-Pistachio Kulfi Pops

*Kulfi is a popular Indian frozen dessert. It's similar to ice cream, but since it isn't whipped, it's much denser and creamier. Pistachio and mango are common flavors, and since I love them both, I decided to combine them into a single kulfi. I like serving it in the form of frosty ice pops—these couldn't be more perfect for an oppressively hot summer day.*

2 large or 4 small mangoes, peeled, seeded, and chopped (about 2 cups chopped flesh)

1/2 cup pistachios, soaked for 2 to 4 hours and drained

1/2 cup coconut milk (page 28)

1 tablespoon lemon juice

1/4 teaspoon sea salt

30 drops liquid stevia (or equivalent sweetener of choice; see page 12), or to taste

YIELD: 6 SERVINGS

**Per serving**: 115 calories, 5.9g fat (1.5g sat), 15.2g carbs, 2g fiber, 2.7g protein

• Grain-Free
• Lower-Fat
• Nut-Free Variation
• Oil-Free
• No Added Sugars

Combine all ingredients in a high-speed blender and blend until smooth. Transfer the mixture to popsicle molds and freeze for several hours, until solid. Remove from the freezer a few minutes before serving.

## SUBSTITUTIONS
- Fresh mangoes: 2 cups thawed frozen mango chunks
- Pistachios: cashews or macadamia nuts
- Coconut milk: nondairy milk of choice (see pages 25-28)
- Lemon juice: lime juice

## VARIATION
- Nut-Free Mango Kulfi: Replace the pistachios with sunflower seeds or 1/4 cup coconut butter (page 36).

**Chef's Tips:** Champagne or ataulfo mangoes are my favorite type to use in this recipe. If you don't have popsicle molds, you can freeze the mixture in small paper cups; simply insert a popsicle stick in the center about 1 hour into the freezing time.

# Dark Chocolate Sorbet

*Naturally low in fat, sorbet is a frozen dessert made with water instead of milk or cream. I was always under the impression that sorbet had to be fruity-flavored—until I encountered chocolate sorbet. This delectable sorbetto di cioccolato is both rich and light at the same time.*

2 cups water
1 cup coconut nectar
1 cup cacao powder
2 teaspoons vanilla extract
1/4 teaspoon sea salt
2 medium, very ripe bananas, peeled
1 tablespoon vodka (optional)

YIELD: 8 SERVINGS

**Per serving**: 160 calories, 1.5g fat (1g sat), 37.8g carbs, 4g fiber, 2.2g protein

• *Grain-Free*
• *Lower-Fat*
• *Nut-Free*
• *Oil-Free*
• *Lower-Sugar Variation*

**Chef's Tip:** I know this recipe calls for a *lot* of coconut nectar, so please feel free (as always) to sub in a less expensive liquid sweetener. You could also use 1/2 cup of coconut nectar plus 1/2 cup maple syrup or agave to help cut the cost!

Combine all ingredients in a high-speed blender and blend until smooth. Transfer the mixture to an ice cream maker and freeze according to the manufacturer's directions.

If you don't own an ice cream maker, pour the blended mixture into a glass bowl or container and place straight into the freezer. Come back to stir the mixture vigorously every 30 minutes or so for 2 to 3 hours, until it has frozen and taken on an ice-cream-like consistency.

## SUBSTITUTIONS
- Coconut nectar: maple syrup, agave nectar, or any other liquid sweetener
- Cacao powder: unsweetened cocoa powder

## VARIATIONS
- Lower-Sugar Chocolate Sorbet: Reduce the water to 1 1/2 cups and replace the coconut nectar with 1 1/2 cups Date Syrup (page 38).
- Chocolate Almond Sorbet: Blend in 1/2 teaspoon almond extract.
- Mocha Sorbet: Replace the water with brewed coffee, or blend in 2 teaspoons instant coffee granules or 1 teaspoon coffee extract.
- Mint Chocolate Sorbet: Reduce the vanilla extract to 1 teaspoon and blend in 1 teaspoon peppermint extract.

# Banana Soft-Serve

*I'm eternally grateful to whoever first came up with the idea to blend frozen bananas into soft-serve ice cream. You don't need an ice cream maker to prepare it, and you can jazz it up in a zillion different ways (see box below for ideas). Best of all, you really only need a single ingredient to make this frosty, low-fat treat. (See photo on page 155.)*

4 medium, *very* ripe bananas, peeled, cut into chunks, and frozen overnight
2 to 4 tablespoons water or nondairy milk of choice (pages 25-28), or as needed

YIELD: 2 LARGE OR 4 SMALL SERVINGS

**Per large serving** (about 1 cup): 195 calories, 1g fat (trace sat), 49.8g carbs, 5.5g fiber, 2.2g protein

**Per small serving** (about 1/2 cup): 98 calories, .5g fat (trace sat), 24.9g carbs, 3g fiber, 1.1g protein

• 20 Minutes or Less
• Grain-Free
• Lower-Fat
• Nut-Free
• Oil-Free
• No Added Sugars

**Chef's Tip:** I keep a stash of peeled, frozen ripe bananas in my freezer at all times so I can whip up smoothies or banana soft-serve anytime I want.

Remove your frozen banana chunks from the freezer 5 to 10 minutes before you plan to make the ice cream to partially defrost them.

Place the banana chunks in a food processor and pulse and blend until smooth and whipped. This may take 5 minutes or more. You can add water or milk, 1 tablespoon at a time, as needed to help the mixture blend smoothly. (Just err on the side of too little rather than too much; you don't want to make banana soup!). Stop blending often to scrape down the sides of the bowl and make sure all the chunks are getting puréed. Serve immediately.

## GOING BANANAS

Though this is delicious with nothing but bananas, I often like to add a pinch of salt and few drops of lemon juice to brighten up the bananas' natural sweetness. My favorite way to eat a bowl is to pour Sugar-Free Chocolate Ganache (page 194) on top—it forms a sort of "magic shell" that you get to break through with your spoon and enjoy with the ice cream. The Fat-Free Chocolate Syrup (page 195) is another great topping option, as is warmed almond butter (page 33), chopped Easy Chocolate Bar (page 166), or fresh berries. Sometimes I even blend in a scoop of nondairy protein powder. On top of all that, you can also blend other frozen fruit in with the bananas to make different flavors of soft-serve—try mangoes or cherries. The possibilities are truly endless.

# Gelato di Avocado

*Buttery, unctuous avocado makes an unbelievably yummy base for raw ice cream. You may wish to use another sweetener in place of the stevia in this gelato if you're particularly sensitive to the taste of avocado and/or stevia.*

2 cups coconut milk (page 28) or nondairy milk of choice (pages 25-28)
3 medium, ripe avocados, pitted, peeled, and chopped (about 2 1/2 cups chopped flesh)
1 tablespoon lemon juice
1/4 teaspoon pure stevia powder (or 1/2 cup liquid sweetener of choice), or to taste
1/4 teaspoon sea salt
1 tablespoon vodka (optional)

YIELD: 6 SERVINGS

Per serving: 132 calories, 12.5g fat (4g sat), 5.9g carbs, 4g fiber, 1.6g protein

• Grain-Free
• Nut-Free
• Oil-Free
• No Added Sugars

**Chef's Tip:** For a more vibrant green color, blend in a small handful of fresh spinach leaves.

Combine all ingredients in a high-speed blender and blend until smooth. Transfer the mixture to an ice cream maker and freeze according to the manufacturer's directions.

## SUBSTITUTION
■ Lemon juice: lime juice

## VARIATIONS
■ Chocolate Avocado Gelato: Blend in 1/4 cup cacao powder or unsweetened cocoa powder.
■ Mint Chip Avocado Gelato: Blend in 1 teaspoon peppermint extract and add 1/3 cup (or more) cacao nibs or nondairy chocolate chips to the ice cream maker near the end of the freezing time.

# Adventures in Candyland

||||||||||||||||||||||||||||||||||||||||||||||||||||||||||||||||||||||||||||||||||||||||||||||||||||||||

## Chocolates, Candies, Fudge, Truffles

*I*'ve always been a little perplexed by the idea of candy—how exactly do you define it? I suppose the best I can do is to say that "candy" must be any dessert enjoyed in roughly bite-sized pieces. That offers plenty of room for variation and experimentation!

Forget the junk you see on store shelves—my raw candies provide both indulgence and nutrients. Chocolate, vanilla, caramel, nuts and seeds, fruit, coconut...you name it, it's here, in all its full-flavored, unadulterated, unprocessed glory. Whether you were a peanut-butter-cup addict or chocolate-kiss fanatic in a former life, I promise you there is a healthy raw substitute to satisfy your candy cravings.

In this chapter you'll find chocolates, truffles, fudge, energy balls, and other poppable, no-bake confections that are easy to make and even easier to devour one after another.

Coconut Butter Fudge (page 170)

# Easy Chocolate Bar

*Not only is this homemade chocolate bar perfect for snacking on out-of-hand, it also makes a great addition to many other recipes in this book. I almost always have a bar or two stashed in my freezer for "chocolate emergencies."*

1 cup melted cacao butter
1/2 cup cacao powder
1/3 cup maple syrup
1 teaspoon vanilla extract
Big pinch of sea salt

YIELD: 16 SERVINGS

**Per serving**: 144 calories, 14g fat (8g sat), 5.9g carbs, 1g fiber, .5g protein

- Grain-Free
- Nut-Free

**Chef's Tip:** If you don't have chocolate molds, you can chill the chocolate in muffin cups (silicone ones work nicely here) or a loaf pan instead.

Combine all ingredients in a high-speed blender and blend on low to combine, then blend on high until completely smooth. (Alternatively, thoroughly whisk all ingredients together in a medium bowl.) Pour the mixture into chocolate molds (any shape of your choice, though I like classic bar molds). Refrigerate for at least 4 hours or freeze for at least 2 hours before popping out of the molds and using or eating.

Store the chocolate in an airtight container (or wrapped tightly in aluminum foil) in the refrigerator for up to a month or in the freezer for up to 3 months.

**SUBSTITUTIONS**
- Cacao powder: unsweetened cocoa powder
- Maple syrup: coconut nectar, agave nectar, or any other liquid sweetener

**VARIATIONS**
- Easy Freezer Chocolate: Replace the cacao butter with coconut oil; the resulting chocolate will melt much more easily, so be sure to store it in the freezer.
- Mix-In Chocolate: Jazz up your chocolate by stirring in maca or mesquite powder, soaked goji berries, cacao nibs, ground coffee beans, or finely chopped nuts before pouring into the molds.

# Salted Tahini Caramels

*There are two types of people in this world: those that adore tahini enough to eat it straight out of the jar, and those that do not. I am of the former persuasion. If you are too, you'll love these tahini-rific little freezer caramels. Have all the ingredients ready to go at room temperature to make for easy mixing.*

1/2 cup tahini
1/4 cup coconut flour
1/4 cup coconut nectar
1/8 teaspoon coarse sea salt

**YIELD: 16** SMALL CARAMELS

**Per caramel:** 64 calories, 4.2g fat (1g sat), 6.1g carbs, 1g fiber, 1.6g protein

- *Grain-Free*
- *Lower-Fat*
- *Nut-Free*

Combine the tahini, coconut flour, and coconut nectar in a medium bowl and stir until very well-mixed (the mixture will be thick). Pour into a small glass container (lined with plastic wrap or waxed paper for easy removal, if desired) or divide between mini muffin cups. Sprinkle evenly with the sea salt and freeze until very firm. Once frozen, slice into bite-sized pieces with a very sharp knife. Enjoy straight out of the freezer.

Store the caramels in an airtight container in the freezer for up to 3 months.

## SUBSTITUTION

- Coconut nectar: agave nectar, maple syrup, or any other liquid sweetener

# Coconut Butter Fudge

*This recipe is criminally simple and endlessly scrumptious.*

2/3 cup coconut butter (page 36)
2 tablespoons coconut nectar
1/8 teaspoon sea salt

**YIELD:** 9 SERVINGS

**Per serving:** 122 calories, 10.8g fat (10g sat), 6.8g carbs, 3g fiber, 1.1g protein

- 20 Minutes or Less
- Grain-Free
- Nut-Free
- Oil-Free
- Lower-Sugar Variation

Warm the coconut butter in a dehydrator or on the stove over very low heat until softened and liquidy. Add the coconut nectar and salt and stir vigorously to combine. The mixture will be thick. Pour into a small glass container (lined with plastic wrap or waxed paper for easy removal, if desired) or divide between mini muffin cups and refrigerate until firm. Once chilled, slice into small squares with a very sharp knife.

Store in an airtight container in the refrigerator for up to 2 weeks or in the freezer for up to 2 months.

**SUBSTITUTION**
- Coconut nectar: agave nectar, maple syrup, or any other liquid sweetener

**VARIATIONS**
- Lower-Sugar Coconut Fudge: Replace the coconut nectar with 3 tablespoons Date Syrup (page 38).
- Flavored Coconut Fudge: Add 1/2 teaspoon of your favorite flavor extract, such as vanilla, almond, or peppermint.

# Cocoa Crunch Clusters

*With just three ingredients plus a pinch of salt, these crunchy, nut-free snacks can be put together in a jiffy. The key is to use a 3:2:1 ratio of raisins:coconut:cacao nibs.*

1 1/2 cups raisins
1 cup unsweetened shredded
  or flaked coconut
1/2 cup cacao nibs
Big pinch of sea salt

**Yield:** about 20 small or 12 large clusters

**Per serving** (if 20): 92 calories, 5.7g fat (4g sat), 11.9g carbs, 3g fiber, 1.6g protein

**Per serving** (if 12): 153 calories, 9.4g fat (7g sat), 19.9g carbs, 5g fiber, 2.6g protein

• *20 Minutes or Less*
• *Grain-Free*
• *Lower-Fat*
• *Nut-Free*
• *Oil-Free*
• *No Added Sugars*

**Chef's Tip:** Instead of rolling these into balls, try pressing them into a pan and cutting them into cubes or bars instead.

Combine all ingredients in a food processor and pulse until the mixture is sticky and well-combined. Roll into balls of any size and refrigerate until firm.

Store in an airtight container at room temperature for up to a week, in the refrigerator for up to 3 weeks, or in the freezer for up to 3 months. If frozen, bring them to room temperature before serving.

**SUBSTITUTION**

■ Raisins: dried cherries, golden raisins, or 1 1/4 cups pitted dates

# Classic Cacao Truffles

*Who doesn't love a good truffle? You can roll these silky-smooth beauties in just about anything you want. I particularly like the color contrast and flavor pairing of chocolate + pistachio.*

1/2 cup cashew butter (page 35)
1/4 cup melted cacao butter
1/4 cup maple syrup
1/2 teaspoon vanilla extract
Big pinch of sea salt
1/4 cup cacao powder
3 tablespoons water
Cacao nibs, unsweetened shredded coconut, and/or crushed pistachios, for rolling (optional)

YIELD: **14** TRUFFLES

**Per truffle**: 109 calories, 8.8g fat (3g sat), 7.3g carbs, 1g fiber, 2g protein

- *Grain-Free*
- *Nut-Free Variation*

**Chef's Tip:** If the mixture gets too warm as you're rolling it into balls, place it back in the fridge for 10 to 20 minutes to firm it up.

In a high-speed blender or food processor, combine the cashew butter, cacao butter, maple syrup, vanilla, and salt. Blend to combine. Add the cacao powder and blend on low (or pulse) until just combined. Turn the machine on and pour in the water in a thin stream; blend until smooth. Transfer the mixture to a small bowl and place in the freezer for 1 hour or in the refrigerator for about 4 hours, until firm.

When the mixture has firmed up, use a spoon to scoop out about 2 teaspoons at a time. Roll the 2-teaspoon scoops into balls, place on a plate lined with wax paper, and chill until firm. Roll the finished truffles in the coating of your choice.

Store the truffles in an airtight container in the refrigerator for up to 2 weeks or in the freezer for up to 2 months.

## SUBSTITUTIONS
- Cashew butter: almond butter (page 33)
- Cacao butter: coconut oil (truffles will lose some of their firmness and flavor)
- Maple syrup: coconut nectar, agave nectar, or any other liquid sweetener
- Cacao powder: unsweetened cocoa powder or carob powder

## VARIATIONS
- Nut-Free Cacao Truffles: Replace the cashew butter with sunseed butter (page 37) or coconut butter (page 36).
- Nutella Truffles: Replace the water with hazelnut liqueur or add 1/2 teaspoon hazelnut extract.
- Superfood Truffles: Roll the truffles in lucuma, maca, or mesquite powder. Optionally, you could also blend a teaspoon of spirulina or your favorite greens powder into the truffles.

Classic Cacao Truffles (opposite)

White Chocolate Vanilla Bean Truffles (page 174)

Lemon Poppyseed Truffles (page 175)

Jingle Balls (page 176)

# White Chocolate Vanilla Bean Truffles

*I'm a fiend for white chocolate, and these truffles deliver the flavor magic of cocoa butter + vanilla in a bite-sized, low-glycemic package. Even avowed white chocolate skeptics will love these. (See photo page 173.)*

1/2 cup cashew butter (page 35)
1/4 cup melted cacao butter
1/4 cup coconut nectar
Seeds from 1/2 vanilla bean
1/8 teaspoon sea salt
2 to 3 tablespoons nondairy milk of choice (pages 25-28)
20 drops liquid stevia (or equivalent sweetener of choice; see page 12) or to taste (optional)
Lucuma or cacao powder, for rolling (optional)

YIELD: 12 TRUFFLES

**Per truffle:** 124 calories, 10g fat (4g sat), 7.5g carbs, .5g fiber, 2g protein

• *Grain-Free*
• *Nut-Free Variation*

**Chef's Tip:** If the mixture gets too warm as you're rolling it into balls, place it back in the fridge for 10 to 20 minutes to firm it up.

In a high-speed blender or food processor, combine the cashew butter, cacao butter, coconut nectar, vanilla, and salt. Blend to combine. Turn the machine on and pour in the milk in a thin stream, adding only as much as is necessary to blend until smooth. Taste for sweetness and add stevia, if desired. Transfer the mixture to a small bowl and place in the freezer for 1 hour or in the refrigerator for about 4 hours, until firm.

When the mixture has firmed up, use a spoon to scoop out about 2 teaspoons at a time. Roll the 2-teaspoon scoops into balls, place on a plate lined with wax paper, and chill until firm. Roll the finished truffles in lucuma or cacao powder, if desired.

Store the truffles in an airtight container in the refrigerator for up to 2 weeks or in the freezer for up to 2 months.

## SUBSTITUTIONS
- Cashew butter: almond butter (page 33)
- Coconut nectar: agave nectar, maple syrup, or any other liquid sweetener
- Vanilla bean: 1 1/2 teaspoons vanilla extract
- Cacao butter: coconut oil (truffles will lose some of the white chocolate flavor)

## VARIATIONS
- Nut-Free White Chocolate Truffles: Replace the cashew butter with coconut butter (page 36).
- Crunchy-Coated White Chocolate Truffles: You can roll the finished truffles in a variety of coatings besides lucuma or cacao powder. Try unsweetened shredded coconut, chopped pistachios, or cacao nibs.

# Lemon Poppyseed Truffles

*These poppable "truffles" were inspired by my dear friend Hannah of wayfaringchocolate.com. They contain no nuts or added sugars and just the right amount of citrusy tang. (See photo page 173.)*

1/2 cup dry sunflower seeds

1/2 cup coconut butter (page 36)

1 1/2 tablespoons lemon juice

1 tablespoon poppyseeds

1/2 teaspoon lemon zest (optional)

1/8 teaspoon sea salt

1/3 cup pitted dates

10 drops liquid stevia (or equivalent sweetener of choice; see page 12), or to taste (optional)

YIELD: 18 TRUFFLES

**Per serving**: 76 calories, 6g fat (4g sat), 5.6g carbs, 2g fiber, 1.3g protein

- 20 Minutes or Less
- Grain-Free
- Lower-Fat
- Nut-Free
- Oil-Free
- No Added Sugars

Place the sunflower seeds in the bowl of a food processor and pulse until coarsely ground. Add the coconut butter, lemon juice and zest, poppyseeds, and salt. Pulse until uniformly combined. Add the dates and pulse just until the mixture begins to stick together slightly (try not to overprocess). You can add water, a teaspoon at a time, if needed to help it come together. Taste the mixture for sweetness, and if it's too tart for your taste, pulse in a bit of stevia.

Scoop up the dough by heaping teaspoonfuls and roll each portion into a ball shape. Place t he rolled truffles onto a plate and refrigerate until firm, 1 to 2 hours.

Store the truffles in an airtight container in the refrigerator for up to a week or in the freezer for up to a month.

## SUBSTITUTIONS
- Sunflower seeds: cashews or almonds
- Dates: 1/2 cup soft golden raisins

## VARIATIONS
- Even-Lower-Fat Poppyseeed Truffles: Replace 1/4 cup of the sunflower seeds with old-fashioned rolled oats; you may need to add an extra date or two to get the mixture sticky.
- Orange Poppyseed Truffles: Replace the lemon juice and zest with orange juice and zest.

# Jingle Balls

*These nut-free snack balls remind me of the holidays with their festive red and green spots! (See photo page 173.)*

1/2 cup dry sunflower seeds
1/2 cup dry pumpkins seeds
1/8 teaspoon sea salt
1/3 cup dried cranberries
1/4 cup soft golden raisins
1/3 cup pitted dates

YIELD: ABOUT 15 BALLS

**Per serving**: 80 calories, 4.7g fat (1g sat), 9.7g carbs, 1g fiber, 2.2g protein

- *20 Minutes or Less*
- *Grain-Free*
- *Lower-Fat*
- *Nut-Free*
- *Oil-Free*
- *No Added Sugars*

In a food processor, combine the sunflower seeds, pumpkin seeds, and salt and process into coarse crumbs. Add the cranberries and raisins, and pulse until uniformly incorporated. Add the dates and pulse just until the mixture begins to stick together (try not to overprocess).

Scoop up the dough, about 2 heaping teaspoons at a time, and roll each portion into a ball shape. Enjoy immediately, or place the balls onto a plate and refrigerate until firm, 1 to 2 hours.

Store in an airtight container at room temperature for up to 4 days, in the refrigerator for up to 2 weeks, or in the freezer for up to 2 months.

## SUBSTITUTIONS

- Sunflower seeds: almonds or Brazil nuts
- Pumpkin seeds: pistachios
- Dried cranberries: dried cherries or soaked goji berries
- Golden raisins: dark raisins or additional dried cranberries

## VARIATIONS

- Even-Lower-Fat Jingle Balls: Replace 1/4 cup of the pumpkin seeds with old-fashioned rolled oats; you may need to add an extra date or two to get the mixture sticky.
- Nutty Jingle Balls: Use almonds and pistachios in place of sunflower and pumpkin seeds, respectively.
- Spiced Jingle Balls: Add 1/4 teaspoon ground cinnamon for more holiday flair.

# Turtle Bites

*I encase sweet, oozy caramel in a sugar-free chocolate shell and top it with crunchy raw pecans in these "turtle" treats.*

1/2 cup cacao powder
1/2 cup melted cacao butter
30 drops liquid stevia (or equivalent sweetener of choice; see page 12)
Pinch of sea salt
1/2 batch Ooey Gooey Caramel Sauce (page 191)
18 dry pecan halves

YIELD: 18 TURTLES

**Per turtle:** 96 calories, 8.6g fat (4g sat), 5.8g carbs, 1g fiber, .8g protein

- *Grain-Free*
- *Nut-Free Variation*
- *No Added Sugars*

**Chef's Tips:** If the chocolate mixture begins to firm up before you're done using it, stick it in a warm dehydrator for a few minutes to melt it back down. A squeeze bottle makes an easy and efficient way to dole out the melted chocolate and/or the caramel sauce. If you have silicone mini muffin cups, use those here.

Line 18 cups of a mini muffin tin with paper liners. In a small bowl, whisk together the cacao powder, cacao butter, stevia, and salt until smooth. Spoon 1 to 2 teaspoons of the chocolate mixture into each muffin cup (just enough to completely cover the bottom). Set the remaining chocolate mixture aside in a warm place. Place the pan in the freezer for about 5 minutes, until the chocolate is solid.

Remove the muffin tin from the freezer and spoon about 1/2 teaspoon Ooey Gooey Caramel Sauce into the center of each cup, gently spreading it into an even layer. Place a pecan half onto each turtle. Spoon 1 to 2 more teaspoons of the remaining chocolate mixture onto each turtle to cover the caramel and nuts. Refrigerate or freeze until firm and set.

Store in an airtight container in the refrigerator for up to 2 weeks or in the freezer for up to 2 months.

## SUBSTITUTION
- Cacao powder: unsweetened cocoa powder or carob powder

## VARIATIONS
- Nut-Free Turtle Bites: Replace the pecans in each turtle bite with a sprinkle of sunflower seeds, pumpkin seeds, hempseeds, or unsweetened flaked coconut.
- Turtle Cups: Use a regular-size muffin tin instead of a mini one to make larger turtles.

# Almond Butter Melties

*This melt-in-your-mouth almond "fudge" is quick to make and addictively tasty. Have all the ingredients at room temperature to make for easy mixing.*

1 cup almond butter (page 33)
2 tablespoons melted coconut oil
2 tablespoons coconut nectar
1/4 teaspoon sea salt

**YIELD: 12** SERVINGS

**Per serving**: 155 calories, 12.9g fat (3g sat), 6.2g carbs, 3g fiber, 4.7g protein

• *20 Minutes or Less*
• *Grain-Free*
• *Nut-Free Variation*
• *Lower-Sugar Variation*

Combine all ingredients in a medium bowl and stir vigorously until well-combined. The mixture will be thick. Pour into a small glass container (lined with plastic wrap or waxed paper for easy removal, if desired) or divide between mini muffin cups and freeze until firm. Once frozen, slice into bite-sized pieces with a very sharp knife. Enjoy straight out of the freezer.

Store in an airtight container in the freezer for up to 3 months.

## SUBSTITUTIONS

- Almond butter: cashew butter (page 35), peanut butter, or any other nut butter
- Coconut nectar: maple syrup, agave nectar, or any other liquid sweetener

## VARIATIONS

- Nut-Free Butter Melties: Replace the almond butter with Sunseed Butter (page 37).
- Lower-Sugar Almond Melties: Replace the coconut nectar with 3 tablespoons Date Syrup (page 38).
- Cinnamon-Almond Melties: Stir 1/4 teaspoon ground cinnamon into the mixture.

# Superfood Snackers

*You can keep these in the freezer almost indefinitely, and reach for one anytime you need an energy boost. I like to pop a couple right before or after a workout.*

1 cup dry walnuts
1/4 cup hempseeds
1/4 cup dry Brazil nuts
1 tablespoon açaí powder
1 to 2 teaspoons greens powder (such as wheatgrass, chlorella, spirulina, etc.)
1 teaspoon maca powder
1/8 teaspoon sea salt
2/3 cup diced dried figs (about 4 large figs)
1/4 cup goji berries (soaked in warm water for 5 to 10 minutes and drained)
1/4 cup dried mulberries
1/3 cup pitted dates

YIELD: 25 BITE-SIZE CUBES

**Per cube:** 79 calories, 5g fat (1g sat), 7.6g carbs, 1g fiber, 2.1g protein

- *20 Minutes or Less*
- *Grain-Free*
- *Lower-Fat*
- *Nut-Free Variation*
- *Oil-Free*
- *No Added Sugars*

**Chef's Tip:** Instead of pressing into a pan and cutting into cubes, try rolling these into balls.

In a food processor, combine the walnuts, hempseeds, Brazil nuts, açaí powder, greens powder, maca powder, and salt. Pulse until the nuts are coarsely ground. Add the diced figs, goji berries, and mulberries and pulse until uniformly incorporated. Add the dates and pulse until the mixture becomes sticky (try not to overprocess).

Press the mixture firmly and evenly into a 6- to 8-inch square baking pan (lined with plastic wrap or waxed paper for easy removal, if desired) and score into small cubes. Enjoy immediately, or place the pan in the refrigerator or freezer to chill and firm up for a couple hours before cutting and snacking.

Store the cubes in an airtight container in the refrigerator for up to 3 weeks or in the freezer for up to 3 months.

## SUBSTITUTIONS

- Walnuts, Brazil nuts, hempseeds: 1 1/2 cups mixed nuts and/or seeds of your choice
- Açaí, greens, maca powders: 1 1/2 to 2 tablespoons powdered superfoods of your choice, such as cacao, camu camu, maqui berry, mesquite, pomegranate, etc.
- Figs: raisins, or additional 1/2 cup pitted dates
- Mulberries: dried goldenberries, golden raisins, or dried cranberries
- Dates: soft raisins

## VARIATIONS

- Even-Lower-Fat Superfood Snackers: Replace 1/3 cup of the walnuts with old-fashioned rolled oats; you may also need to pulse in an extra date or two to help the mixture stick together.
- Nut-Free Superfood Snackers: Replace the walnuts with sunflower seeds (for vitamin E) and the Brazil nuts with pumpkin seeds (for zinc).
- Super Protein Snackers: Omit the superfood powders (açaí, greens, and maca) and add 2 tablespoons of your favorite nondairy protein powder.

## SUPERFOODS: KEEP 'EM IN MIND

I have a whole pantry shelf full of fun and exciting superfoods, but since I like to create fairly simple and accessible recipes, I only rarely use them in my recipe development. I wanted to provide you with at least one super-powered treat here, though! These little cubes are packed with nutritional goodies: essential omega-3 fats from walnuts and hempseeds, selenium from Brazil nuts, antioxidants from açaí, alkalizing chlorophyll from greens powder, hormone-stabilizing adaptogens from maca, trace minerals from sea salt, calcium from figs, vitamin C and amino acids from gojis and mulberries, and finally potassium and fiber from dates. Told ya they were super-powered!

# Cashew Butter Cups

*If you've ever been a fan of a certain orange-wrapped peanut butter cup, you'll love this layered candy. The nutritional yeast is completely optional, but it gives the filling a certain* je ne sais quoi *that rounds out the buttery flavor in a magical way.*

**Chocolate:**
1/2 cup melted cacao butter
6 tablespoons cacao powder
1/4 cup maple syrup
1/2 teaspoon vanilla extract
Pinch of sea salt

**Filling:**
1/3 cup cashew butter (page 35)
2 tablespoons maple syrup
2 tablespoons nondairy milk of choice (pages 25-28)
1 teaspoon nutritional yeast (optional)

YIELD: 12 CANDIES

**Per truffle:** 157 calories, 13.1g fat (6g sat), 10.3g carbs, 1g fiber, 2g protein

- *Grain-Free*
- *Nut-Free Variation*

**Chocolate:** Combine the cacao butter and powder, maple syrup, vanilla, and salt in a small bowl. Whisk until very smooth. Spoon half the chocolate mixture, 1 to 2 teaspoons at a time (depending on the size of your molds), into deep, round chocolate molds *or* mini muffin cups lined with paper liners. Gently tap the pan on the counter to level out the chocolate. (The bottoms of your molds should now have a thin, uniform layer of chocolate.) Place the mold or pan in the freezer for a minutes while you make the filling. Set the remaining half of the chocolate mixture aside in a warm place.

**Filling:** Stir the cashew butter, maple syrup, milk, and nutritional yeast (if using) together in another small bowl. Remove the mold or pan from the freezer and carefully spoon the cashew butter mixture, about a teaspoon at a time, on top of the chocolate layer in each cup. Gently tap the pan on the counter to level out the filling layer. Place the mold or pan back in the freezer for 5 minutes.

To finish the candies, remove the mold or pan from the freezer again and carefully spoon the remaining half of the chocolate mixture, 1 to 2 teaspoons at a time, on top of the filling in each cup. Gently tap the pan on the counter to level out the chocolate, if needed. Place the mold or pan back in the freezer and chill for at least one hour, until firm.

Store the finished candies in an airtight container in the freezer for up to 2 months.

**SUBSTITUTIONS**
- Cacao butter: coconut oil (candies will lose some of their flavor and melt more quickly)
- Maple syrup: coconut nectar, agave nectar, or any other liquid sweetener
- Cacao powder: unsweetened cocoa powder or carob powder

**VARIATIONS**

- Nut-Free Butter Cups: Replace the cashew butter with coconut butter (page 36), sunseed butter (page 37), or even tahini.
- Other-Nut Butter Cups: Replace the cashew butter with almond butter (page 33), macadamia nut butter (reducing the milk to 1 tablespoon), or even natural creamy peanut butter.

# Chocolate Protein Bark

*Coconut oil's medium-chain fatty acids are converted into energy rather than body fat, making it a healthy oil and a good choice for pre-workout fuel, especially when combined with easily-absorbable plant-based protein. You'll definitely want to use a protein powder that you love the taste of on its own, as its flavor will be prominent in this candy.*

1/3 cup melted coconut oil

1 1/2 scoops (about 30 grams) chocolate-flavored nondairy protein powder of choice

1 teaspoon mesquite or maca powder (optional)

Stevia to taste (or equivalent sweetener of choice; see page 12)

Cacao powder, as desired

YIELD: 6 SERVINGS

Per serving: 124 calories, 12.4g fat (10g sat), 1g carbs, .5g fiber, 3.7g protein

*Nutritional values will vary slightly depending on the brand of protein powder used.

- 20 Minutes or Less
- Grain-Free
- Nut-Free
- No Added Sugars

In a small bowl, whisk together the coconut oil, chocolate protein powder, and mesquite or maca (if using). Taste for sweetness and flavor—depending on your brand of protein powder, you may want to add a few drops of stevia or a couple teaspoons cacao powder.

Pour the mixture into a 6- to 8-inch square baking pan lined with waxed paper and place in the freezer to chill for about 30 minutes. Once frozen, break the bark into chunks and enjoy.

Store the protein bark in an airtight container in the freezer for up to 3 weeks.

## SUBSTITUTION
- Cacao powder: unsweetened cocoa powder or carob powder

## VARIATION
- Vanilla-Almond Protein Bark: Use a vanilla-flavored protein powder and add a few drops of almond extract.

**Chef's Tip:** If you include the mesquite or maca powder, you may find that the mixture separates a bit while freezing, but this doesn't affect the taste at all.

# To Top It All Off

*I* used to watch, baffled, as my dad would scrape the frosting off a slice of cake and discard it to the side of his plate. When my horror abated, I would reach over and help myself to the sweet fluff he'd abandoned. I'm sure I'm not the only one who's ever thought the icing was the best part of a dessert! As I got older and wiser, though, the idea of eating a big glob of hydrogenated fat and processed sugars appealed less and less to me.

Enter: raw frostings and fillings. Now you can complement your cakes with whole-food frostings, top your brownies with drizzly syrups, and pack your pastries with gooey or fruity fillings, none of which contain a speck of anything artificial. With these recipes, you can have your cake and eat (the frosting) too—guilt-free.

Included in this chapter are all the icings, fillings, frostings, glazes, syrups, drizzles, and ganaches you'll need to crown many of the other desserts in this book. That said – just between you and me – I won't tell anybody if you make one of these recipes just to eat it with a spoon.

Fruity Chia Jam (page 196)

# Vanilla-Coconut Crème

*As far as I'm concerned, this is the queen of luscious raw icings. I challenge you to dollop it on just about anything in this book and not go bonkers over it. Believe it or not, it makes a great dessert all by itself—simply pour it into some small ramekins and refrigerate for several hours, and you'll have creamy vanilla-flecked custard at the ready.*

1 cup cashews or macadamia nuts, soaked for 2 to 4 hours and drained

1/2 cup water or coconut water

1/4 cup coconut butter (page 36)

1 teaspoon lemon juice

1/8 teaspoon sea salt

Seeds from 1/2 vanilla bean or 1 1/2 teaspoons vanilla extract

30 drops liquid stevia (or equivalent sweetener of choice; see page 12)

YIELD: 12 SERVINGS (ABOUT 1 1/2 CUPS)

**Per serving** (2 tablespoons): 96 calories, 8.2g fat (4g sat), 4.7g carbs, 1g fiber, 2.5g protein

• Grain-Free
• Lower-Fat Variation
• Oil-Free
• No Added Sugars

Combine the soaked cashews, water, coconut butter, lemon juice, salt, vanilla bean, and stevia in a high-speed blender (or a good-quality food processor) and blend until smooth. Taste for sweetness and add additional stevia if desired. Use immediately or refrigerate until ready to use.

Store in a glass jar or airtight container in the refrigerator for up to 3 days.

**VARIATION**

■ Lower-Fat Crème: Replace 1/4 cup of the cashews with plain or vanilla nondairy yogurt, reducing the water to 6 tablespoons.

# Fluffy Chocolate Frosting

*"Fluffy" is really the only way to accurately describe the texture of this frosting. It's firm enough to be piped or piled onto cakes or cupcakes, but light and airy enough to melt in your mouth. Fair warning: you may find yourself eating it by the spoonful. (See cupcake topping in photo, page 108.)*

2 large, ripe avocados, pitted, peeled, and chopped (about 2 cups chopped flesh)
1/2 cup maple syrup
1 teaspoon vanilla extract
1 teaspoon lemon juice
1/8 teaspoon sea salt
1/2 cup cacao powder

YIELD: 16 SERVINGS (ABOUT 2 CUPS)

**Per serving** (2 tablespoons): 62 calories, 3.2g fat (1g sat), 9.5g carbs, 2g fiber, 1g protein

- 20 Minutes or Less
- Grain-Free
- Lower-Fat
- Nut-Free
- Oil-Free

**Chef's Tip:** For a deeper chocolate flavor, blend in an additional 2 tablespoons cacao powder.

Combine the avocados, maple syrup, vanilla, lemon juice, and salt in a food processor. Blend until smooth and combined. Add the cacao powder and blend again until smooth. Refrigerate until ready to use.

Store in a glass jar or airtight container in the refrigerator for up to 3 days.

### SUBSTITUTIONS
- Maple syrup: coconut nectar, agave nectar, or any other liquid sweetener
- Cacao powder: unsweetened cocoa powder or carob powder

### VARIATION
- Fluffy Flavored Frosting: Replace the vanilla extract with 1/2 teaspoon of another flavor extract, such as coffee, hazelnut, or almond.

# Tangy Cream Cheese Icing

*This lightly sweetened icing is perfect on carrot cake (see page 94) or any other dessert that could use a hint of tang. You can find dairy-free probiotic powder at natural food stores or bluebonnet-nutrition.com.*

3/4 cup cashews, soaked for 2 to 4 hours and drained

1/2 cup + 2 tablespoons non-dairy milk of choice (pages 25-28)

1 1/2 teaspoons lemon juice

1/2 teaspoon probiotic powder (see Chef's Tip)

2 tablespoons coconut nectar

Pinch of sea salt

10 drops liquid stevia (or equivalent sweetener of choice; see page 12), or to taste (optional)

**YIELD:** 8 SERVINGS (ABOUT 1 CUP)

**Per serving** (2 tablespoons): 94 calories, 6g fat (1g sat), 8.2g carbs, 1g fiber, 2.6g protein

- Grain-Free
- Lower-Fat Variation
- Oil-Free
- Lower-Sugar Variation

**Chef's Tip:** If you don't have loose probiotic powder, you could empty the powder out of 2 probiotic capsules (discarding the capsules after emptying) and use that instead.

Combine the soaked cashews, nondairy milk, lemon juice, and probiotic powder in a high-speed blender and blend until smooth. You may need to use the tamper. Transfer the mixture to a medium bowl and cover with plastic wrap. Set the bowl in a warm place (such as in a dehydrator set to 110°F, on a sunny windowsill, or on top of the refrigerator) and let the icing culture for 5 to 6 hours.

When the icing has finished culturing, transfer it to a food processor or high-speed blender. Add the coconut nectar and salt and whip until smooth. Alternatively, you can refrigerate the icing after it has cultured and sweeten it the next day. Taste for sweetness and stir in the stevia if desired. Transfer to a bowl or container and refrigerate for at least 2 hours, or until ready to use.

Store in a glass jar or airtight container in the refrigerator for up to 5 days.

## SUBSTITUTIONS
- Cashews: macadamia nuts
- Coconut nectar: agave nectar or any other liquid sweetener

## VARIATIONS
- Lower-Fat Cream Cheese Icing: Replace 1/4 cup of the cashews with plain or vanilla nondairy yogurt and reduce the milk to 1/2 cup.
- Lower-Sugar Cream Cheese Icing: Replace the coconut nectar with 3 tablespoons Date Syrup (page 38).
- Quick Cream Cheese Icing: Omit the probiotic powder, reduce the nondairy milk to 1/2 cup, and skip the culturing step; instead, simply blend all ingredients together until smooth and refrigerate until ready to use.
- Sweet Cream Cheese Icing: Culture the icing for only 3 to 4 hours, then double the amount of coconut nectar or add additional stevia to taste.

(opposite)

# Ooey Gooey Caramel Sauce

*This nearly-fat-free caramel derives its color and sweetness from dates—nature's candy!*

1 cup pitted dates, soaked in warm water for 20 minutes and drained
2/3 cup nondairy milk of choice (see pages 25-28)
1 teaspoon vanilla extract
1/8 teaspoon sea salt

YIELD: 8 SERVINGS (ABOUT 1 CUP)

**Per serving** (2 tablespoons): 74 calories, .2g fat (trace sat), 18.9g carbs, 2g fiber, .6g protein

- *20 Minutes or Less*
- *Grain-Free*
- *Lower-Fat*
- *Nut-Free*
- *Oil-Free*
- *No Added Sugars*

Combine all ingredients in a high-speed blender and blend until smooth.

Store in a glass jar or airtight container in the refrigerator for up to 3 days.

**Chef's Tip:** Almond milk (page 25) or coconut milk (page 28) are my two favorite milks to use in this caramel.

# Raspberry Coulis

*This dessert sauce (pronounced "cool-lee") is tart, fruit, and perfect for drizzling. I like to use frozen raspberries for their year-round availability and affordability, but you're welcome to use fresh berries if you prefer. (See topping on New York Cheesecake, page 105.)*

1 (10-ounce) bag thawed frozen raspberries

2 teaspoons lemon or lime juice

15 to 20 drops liquid stevia (or equivalent sweetener of choice; see page 12), or to taste

Pinch of sea salt

YIELD: 8 SERVINGS (ABOUT 1 CUP)

**Per serving** (2 tablespoons): 15 calories, trace fat (trace sat), 3.3g carbs, 1.5g fiber, .1g protein

• 20 Minutes or Less
• Grain-Free
• Lower-Fat
• Nut-Free
• Oil-Free
• No Added Sugars

Combine all ingredients in a high-speed blender and blend until very smooth. Taste for sweetness and add more stevia if desired. Strain the mixture through a fine-mesh sieve, transfer to a glass jar, and refrigerate until ready to use.

Store in a glass jar or airtight container in the refrigerator for up to 3 days.

**VARIATION**

■ Strawberry Coulis: Replace the raspberries with strawberries, adjusting the amount of stevia as needed.

# Coconut Lemon Curd

*This isn't a jelly-like lemon curd. It has a firm, moldable texture you can scoop up, roll into balls or flatten into discs, and use to top or fill Lemon Love Cupcakes (page 106) or anything else you like. Make sure your coconut butter is softened and liquidy before mixing everything together.*

1 cup coconut butter (page 36)
2 tablespoons lemon juice
1 1/2 tablespoons coconut nectar
1 teaspoon lemon zest
Big pinch of sea salt
Pinch of turmeric (optional), for color

YIELD: 10 SERVINGS (ABOUT 1 1/4 CUPS)

**Per serving** (2 tablespoons): 158 calories, 14.5g fat (13g sat), 7.5g carbs, 4g fiber, 1.6g protein

• 20 Minutes or Less
• Grain-Free
• Nut-Free
• Oil-Free
• Lower-Sugar Variation

Combine all ingredients in a medium bowl and stir vigorously with a fork or spoon to combine. The lemon juice will "curdle" the coconut butter, causing it to seize up slightly—this is normal! Just continue stirring until the mixture smoothes back out. If you're having trouble, you can add melted coconut *oil,* a teaspoon at a time, until it reaches a consistency you're happy with.

Store in a glass jar or airtight container at room temperature for up to 4 days or in the refrigerator for up to 2 weeks. If refrigerated, soften to room temperature before using.

**SUBSTITUTION**
■ Coconut nectar: agave nectar, maple syrup, or any other liquid sweetener

**VARIATIONS**
■ Lower-Sugar Coconut Lemon Curd: Replace the coconut nectar with 2 tablespoons Date Syrup (page 38).
■ Coconut Lime Curd: Replace the lemon juice and zest with lime juice and zest. Key limes would be especially nice here!

# Sugar-Free Chocolate Ganache

*This thick, rich, and versatile fudge sauce is pure decadence on a spoon—yet it's sugar-free! (If you're sensitive to the flavor of stevia, just use your favorite liquid sweetener to make the stevia-free variation below.)*

3/4 cup melted coconut oil
1 teaspoon vanilla extract
1/8 teaspoon pure stevia
   powder (or equivalent
   sweetener of choice; see
   page 12), or to taste
Big pinch of sea salt
1/2 cup cacao powder

**YIELD:** ABOUT 1 CUP

**Per tablesp**oon: 94 calories,
10.5g fat (9g sat), 1.4g carbs,
1g fiber, .5g protein

- 20 Minutes or Less
- Grain-Free
- Nut-Free
- No Added Sugars

Combine the coconut oil, vanilla, stevia, and salt in a high-speed blender. Blend on low to combine. Add the cacao powder and blend again on low speed until smooth. (Alternatively, whisk all ingredients together in a medium bowl until smooth and combined.) Taste for sweetness and add additional stevia if desired. Use immediately or transfer to a glass jar and keep at room temperature until ready to use. The ganache will thicken up as it sits; you can use it as-is for a fudgy frosting, or re-liquefy it by placing the jar in a warm dehydrator or in a bowl of warm water, stirring occasionally.

Store in a glass jar or airtight container at room temperature for up to 4 days or in the refrigerator for up to 2 weeks, bringing to room temperature again before serving.

## SUBSTITUTION
- Cacao powder: unsweetened cocoa powder or carob powder

## VARIATIONS
- Stevia-Free Chocolate Ganache: Replace the stevia with 1/4 cup maple syrup, coconut nectar, or any other liquid sweetener.
- Flavored Chocolate Ganache: Replace the vanilla extract with 1/2 teaspoon of another flavor extract, such as coffee, hazelnut, or almond.

opposite

# Fat-Free Chocolate Syrup

*This drizzly cocoa syrup is full of flavor, despite containing no added fats.*

1/3 cup maple syrup
1/4 cup water
1 teaspoon vanilla extract
1/8 teaspoon sea salt
1/3 cup cacao powder

**YIELD:** 8 SERVINGS (ABOUT 1 CUP)

**Per serving** (2 tablespoons):
43 calories, .5g fat (trace sat),
10.8g carbs, 1g fiber, .7g protein

- 20 Minutes or Less
- Grain-Free
- Lower-Fat
- Nut-Free
- Oil-Free

Combine the maple syrup, water, vanilla, salt in a high-speed blender and blend together. Add the cacao powder and blend on low speed until smooth, adding 1 to 2 tablespoons water as needed. Alternatively, whisk the ingredients together in a medium bowl until smooth and combined. Use immediately or refrigerate until ready to use.

Store in a glass jar or airtight container in the refrigerator for up to a week.

**SUBSTITUTIONS**
- Maple syrup: coconut nectar, agave nectar, or any other liquid sweetener
- Cacao powder: unsweetened cocoa powder or carob powder

**VARIATION**
- Flavored Chocolate Syrup: Replace the vanilla extract with 1/2 teaspoon of another flavor extract, such as coffee, hazelnut, or almond.

# Fruity Chia Jam

*You have two options for this jam: fresh fruit or dried fruit. That way, homemade jam is only a blender-blitz away, even in the dead of winter. White chia seeds are nice here, as they don't affect the appearance of the jam as much, but black ones are perfectly fine to use as well.*

**Fresh fruit version:**
2 cups fresh berries or diced fruit
2 teaspoons lemon juice
Liquid stevia (or equivalent sweetener of choice; see page 12) to taste (optional)
Pinch of sea salt
2 tablespoons chia seeds

*-or-*

**Dried fruit version:**
1 cup dried (preferably unsulfured) fruit, soaked in 1 cup warm water for 30 minutes and drained, soaking water reserved
2 teaspoons lemon juice
Pinch of sea salt
1 tablespoon chia seeds

YIELD: 10 SERVINGS (ABOUT 1 1/4 CUPS)

**Per serving** (2 tablespoons), fresh fruit version: 41 calories, 1.1g fat (trace sat),7.5g carbs, 3g fiber, 1.1g protein

**Per serving** (2 tablespoons), dried version: 47 calories, .4g fat (trace sat), 11g carbs, 2g fiber, .6g protein

- *Grain-Free*
- *Lower-Fat*
- *Nut-Free*
- *Oil-Free*
- *No Added Sugars*

**Fresh fruit version:** Place the fruit, lemon juice, stevia (if desired), and salt in a high-speed blender or mini food processor. Blend until smooth. Scrape down the sides, add the chia seeds, and blend again until smooth. Transfer to a small bowl and let sit at room temperature for 2 to 4 hours, until it thickens up to your liking. Use immediately or transfer to a glass jar or container (leaving an inch or two of room at the top) and refrigerate until ready to use.

**Dried fruit version:** Place the drained fruit, 1/2 cup of the soaking water, lemon juice, and salt in a high-speed blender or mini food processor. Blend until smooth. Add additional soaking water, 1 tablespoon at a time, if needed to help it blend. Scrape down the sides, add the chia seeds, and blend again until smooth. Transfer to a small bowl and let sit at room temperature for 2 to 4 hours, until it thickens up to your liking. Use immediately or transfer to a glass jar or container (leaving an inch or two of room at the top) and refrigerate until ready to use.

Fresh fruit jam can be stored in the refrigerator for up to 3 days. Dried fruit jam can be stored in the refrigerator for up to 5 days.

## VARIATIONS
- Fresh fruit version: Use strawberries, raspberries, blueberries, blackberries, oranges, etc.
- Dried fruit version: Use dried apricots, raisins or golden raisins, cherries, figs, etc.

**Fruity Chia Jam** three ways (left to right): a fresh fruit version made with blueberries; a fresh fruit version made with raspberries; and a dried fruit version made with apricots.

**Chef's Tip:** Depending on which fruit you use in the fresh fruit version, you may not want to add any stevia at all. For example, I find blueberry jam to be sweet enough all by itself, while raspberry jam benefits from a little added sweetness.

# *Resources*

||||||||||||||||||||||||||||||||||||||||||||||||||||||||||||||||||||||||||||||||||||||||||||||||||||||||||||||||||||||||||||

## Ingredients, Equipment, Education

*A*t this point, you may be ready and raring to hop to your kitchen and begin dazzling your family and friends with raw pastries aplenty. If you keep a well-stocked pantry (see chapter 1), go right ahead and do so!

If you're new to raw desserts, you may need a few supplies first. Most of my desserts can be made with a few basic pieces of equipment and ingredients commonly found in grocery stores, but you may be wondering what brands I recommend and where to go if you want to shop online. This chapter contains a list of sources and resources for finding raw food-related items and other helpful information.

# Resources

The companies and sources that follow are my preferences and recommendations for acquiring raw food ingredients, equipment, or supplements, and for finding educational resources.

## Ingredients

### Blue Mountain Organics

**bluemountainorganics.com**

100% organic and truly-raw nuts and seeds, nut and seed butters, sweeteners, dried fruit, coconut products, flours, oats, cacao products, superfoods, vanilla beans, and more, all of superior quality and integrity. My #1 go-to source for raw food ingredients.

### Nuts.com

**nuts.com**

Bulk quantities of organic raw nuts, seeds, dried fruit, coconut/almond/cashew flour, palm sugar, superfood powders, and more. Large selection, great prices, and fast shipping.

### NuNaturals Stevia

**nunaturals.com**

The best-tasting stevia extracts and powders I've ever found. Their Pure Liquid Vanilla Stevia is my favorite.

### Coconut Secret

**coconutsecret.com**

The only source, currently, for raw organic coconut nectar. They also carry coconut crystals (sugar) and flour.

### Navitas Naturals

**navitasnaturals.com**

Superfood powders, exotic dried fruits, cacao powder, raw seeds and nuts, and more.

### Tropical Traditions

**tropicaltraditions.com**

High-quality organic coconut oil, coconut flour, shredded/flaked coconut, maple syrup, and more.

## Frontier Co-op

**frontiercoop.com**

Organic herbs, spices, flavor extracts, and vanilla beans.

## Harmless Harvest

**harmlessharvest.com**

The only source for truly-raw, organic coconut water.

# Equipment

## Vitamix

**vitamix.com**

My high-speed blender of choice. It's worth the price, as it will last a lifetime.

## Blendtec

**blendtec.com**

Another popular high-speed blender option.

## Cuisinart

**cuisinart.com**

I have an 11-cup Cuisinart food processor and a miniature 3-cup one, and I couldn't love them more. Cuisinart also offers excellent ice cream makers.

## KitchenAid

**kitchenaid.com**

Stand mixers by KitchenAid are high-quality and long-lasting. They also make food processors, blenders, and more.

## Tribest Sedona

**tribestlife.com**

My preferred brand of dehydrator, offering digital controls, BPA-free trays, and many other modern features.

## Excalibur

**excaliburdehydrators.com**

Another good brand of dehydrator. I like the models with built-in timers and temperature controls.

## Nesco

**nesco.com**

For aspiring raw foodies on a budget, Nesco dehydrators are inexpensive yet reliable.

## Pure Joy Planet

**purejoyplanet.com**

Nut milk bags with free shipping.

# Protein Powders

## Sunwarrior

**sunwarrior.com**

Raw, organic protein powders. Their Warrior Blend (made of pea, hemp, and cranberry protein) is my favorite.

## PlantFusion

**plantfusion.net**

Hypoallergenic and easy-to-digest powders made of pea, artichoke, sprouted quinoa, and sprouted amaranth proteins.

## Sprout Living

**sproutliving.com**

Their Epic Protein powders are made of the finest brown rice protein available.

## Vega

**myvega.com**

High-quality plant-based protein powders and shakes created by vegan Ironman triathlete Brendan Brazier.

# Education

## Matthew Kenney Academy

**matthewkenneycuisine.com/education**

My "rawlma mater" is the culinary academy of chef Matthew Kenney, my mentor and long-time inspiration. Their classical approach to teaching the art of gourmet living cuisine is unmatched.

## Russell James

**therawchef.com/amber**

As the UK's leading raw chef and my former instructor at the Matthew Kenney Academy, Russell is an expert on all things raw. He offers online chef courses and learn-at-home DVDs.

## Living Light Culinary Arts Institute

**rawfoodchef.com**

Cherie Soria's Living Light is the longest-running raw chef school in the country. Their classes are especially well-suited for anyone interested in becoming a raw food teacher or instructor.

## Uncooking101

**uncooking101.com**

Éva Rawposa is constantly churning out tips, tricks, and educational materials, perfect for raw food newbies or veterans.

# Other Information

## Chef Amber Shea

**chefambershea.com**

My blog is the place where you can find out what I'm up to, check out new recipes as I create them, read about my traveling adventures, say hello or ask a question, and generally interact with me! You can even subscribe to receive my posts by email.

Feel free to follow me on Facebook and Twitter as well: **facebook.com/chefambershea** and **twitter.com/chefambershea**

# Acknowledgments

I'd like to thank my editor, Jon Robertson, and the team at Vegan Heritage Press for believing in my work and creating such beautiful books out of it.

Thank you to my recipe testers for your generous dedication of time and resources to helping me make these recipes the best they can be. Tracy Derry, Rachel Detwieler, Kayti Downey, Verena Geduldig, Janet Malowany, Sarah McPherson, Carol R. Palo, Jennifer M. Robertson, Theodora Wallace, and Mary Crouch Young, thank you for all your hard work.

A special thank you to Blue Mountain Organics, NuNaturals, Navitas Naturals, and Tribest Life for donating ingredients and equipment for my recipe testing purposes.

Thank you to my parents, Ken and Cheryl Ford, for your lifetime of believing in me.

A massive thank you to my husband Matt for your endless love, encouragement, generosity, and positivity. I could not do what I do without you. I promise to keep making you treats forever!

Last but not least, a huge thank you to all my fans and blog readers of chefambershea.com, to whom this book is dedicated. Your readership, interraction, and support mean the world to me. Thank you all!

# About the Author

Amber Shea Crawley is a chef and author who specializes in healthful plant-based food. She was trained in the art of gourmet living cuisine at the world-renowned Matthew Kenney Academy, graduating in 2010 as a certified raw and vegan chef. In 2011, she earned her Nutrition Educator certification at the Living Light Culinary Arts Institute. Amber is also a linguist and the author of *Practically Raw: Flexible Raw Recipes Anyone Can Make.* She lives with her husband Matt in Kansas City, Missouri and blogs at ChefAmberShea.com.

Stephen Melvin

# Index

## A

agave nectar, about, 10
allergies and intolerances, 2
Almond(s):
  about, 4
  Cookies, Cherry, 52
  Butter: about, 7; recipe for, 33
  Butter Banana Cupcakes, 114
  Butter Melties, 178
  Flour: about, 10; recipe for, 29
Apple Pie, Deep-Dish Caramel, 118
Applesauce, Instant, 39
Austrian Sacher Torte, 100

## B

Baklava Blondies, 79
Banana(s):
  Butter Brownies, 68
  -Oat Breakfast Bars, Matt's, 86
  Pudding, Not-Your-Grandma's, 148
  Soft-Serve, 162
bars: See "Cookies and Bars."
Blender, 16
Blondies:
  Baklava, 79
  II, Famous Five-Minute, 73
  Strawberry, 74
  White Chocolate Macadamia Nut, 76
Blueberry Dream Pie, 124
Brazil nuts, 5
Brownies:
  Banana Butter, 68
  Tuxedo Cheesecake, 70

Ultimate Raw, 67
Butter(s): about, 7
  Almond, 33
  Cashew, 35
  Coconut, 36
  Sunseed, 37

## C

Cacao:
  Butter, about, 8
  nibs, about, 8
  powder, about, 8
Cake(s) and Cupcake(s):
  Almond Butter Banana Cupcakes, 114
  Austrian Sacher Torte, 100
  Banana Cupcakes, Almond Butter, 114
  Coconut Heaven Cupcakes, 113
  Confetti Birthday, 90
  Crumb-Topped Chocolate Hazelnut Torte, 102
  Devil's Food Cupcakes, 109
  Enlightened Carrot, 94
  German Chocolate, 92
  Lemon Love Cupcakes, 106
  Maple Streusel Coffee Cake Squares, 97
  New York Cheesecake, 104
  Pineapple Upside-Down, 98
  Strawberry Shortcupcakes, 110
Candy(-ies):
  Almond Butter Melties, 178
  Cashew Butter Cups, 182
  Chocolate Protein Bark, 184
  Classic Cacao Truffles, 173
  Cocoa Crunch Clusters, 171
  Coconut Butter Fudge, 170

Easy Chocolate Bar, 166
Jingle Balls, 176
Lemon Poppyseed Truffles, 175
Salted Tahini Caramels, 169
Superfood Snackers, 180
Turtle Bites, 177
White Chocolate Vanilla Bean Truffles, 174
carob powder, about, 9
Carrot Cake, Enlightened, 94
Cashew(s): about, 5
   butter, about, 7; recipe for, 35
   Butter Cups, 182
   Flour, about, 10; recipe, 30
Cheesecake(s):
   New York, 104
   Brownies, Tuxedo, 70
Cherry:
   Almond Cookies, 52
   -Carob Bars, 84
   Crumbles, Individual, 137
Chewy Oatmeal Raisin Cookies, 50
Chia seeds, about, 5
Chocolate: about, 8
   Bar, Easy, 166
   Cake, German, 92
   chips, nondairy, 9
   Chunk Cookies, 42
   Frosting, Fluffy, 189
   Ganache, Sugar-Free, 194
   Hazelnut Torte, Crumb-Topped, 102
   Mousse, Velvety, 147
   Protein Bark, 184
   Pudding, Sugar-Free, 154
   Sorbet, Dark, 160
   Syrup, Fat-Free, 195
   Truffle Tart with Macaroon Crust, Dark, 130
   Walnut Drop Cookies, 57
Classic Cacao Truffles, 172
Cobbler, Vanilla Bean Peach, 140
Cocoa Crunch Clusters, 171
Coco-Nana Cream Pie, 127
Coconut:

Butter, about 7; recipe for, 36
Butter Fudge, 170
dried, unsweetened, 13
flour, about, 9
Heaven Cupcakes, 113
Lemon Curd, 193
meat, not used, 15
Milk, 28
nectar, 10
oil, about, 7
palm sugar, 11
water, 13
coffee, 14
Confetti Birthday Cake, 90
Cookies and Bars:
   Cherry Almond, 52
   Cherry-Carob Bars, 84
   Chewy Oatmeal Raisin, 50
   Chocolate Chunk, 42
   Chocolate Walnut Drop, 57
   Cutouts, Sugar, 44
   Detox Macaroons, 62
   Goji Berry Granola Bars, 80
   Jam Thumbprint, 58
   Marzipan Buckeye Bars, 82
   Matt's Banana-Oat Breakfast Bars, 86
   Midnight Mocha, 46
   Nutty Buddy Sandwiches, 54
   Pecan Chai Spice Bars, 85
   Pecan Shortbread, 60
   Protein Crinkle, 63
   Russian Tea Cakes, 49
Create-Your-Own Ice Cream, 156
Crumb-Topped Chocolate Hazelnut Torte, 102
cupcakes: See "Cakes and Cupcakes."

**D**

Dark Chocolate Sorbet, 160
Dark Chocolate Truffle Tart with Macaroon
   Crust, 130
dates, as sweeteners, 13
Date Syrup: about, 11; recipe for, 38

Deep-Dish Caramel Apple Pie, 118
dehydrating, 17
dehydrators, 17
Detox Macaroons, 62
Devil's Food Cupcakes, 109
dried fruit, as a sweetener, 11
Dulce de Leche Spooncream, 151

**E**

Easy Chia Pudding, 144
Easy Chocolate Bar, 166
equipment, 16
Enlightened Carrot Cake, 94
enzymes, 2

**F**

Famous Five-Minute Blondies II, 73
Fat-Free Chocolate Syrup, 195
fats, 2
fiber, 2
flavor extracts, 14
flaxseeds, about, 5
Flour(s) and Grain(s): about 9
    Almond, 29
    Cashew, 10, 30
    Instant Almond, 30
    Oat, 32
    Sunflour, 10, 31
Fluffy Chocolate Frosting, 189
food processors, 16
French Silk Pie, 122
frostings: See "Topping(s), Frosting(s), and
    Sauce(s)."
fruits, as sweeteners, 12
Fruity Chia Jam, 196-197

**G**

Gelato di Avocado, 163
German Chocolate Cake, 92
Goji Berry Granola Bars, 80
grains: See "Flours and Grains."

Granola Bars, Goji Berry, 80

**H**

Hazelnuts, about, 5
Hazelnut Torte, Crumb-Topped Chocolate,
    102
Hempseeds, about, 7

**I**

Ice-Cream(s): See "Puddings, Ice Creams,
    and Pops."
    Create-Your-Own, 156
    flavor combos, 157
    makers, 16
Ingredient Guide, 4
Individual Cherry Crumbles, 137
Instant:
    Almond Flour, 30
    Applesauce, 39
    Nut Milk, 26
    Seed Milk, 27
Irish moss gel, not used, 15

**J**

Jam Thumbprint Cookies, 58
Jingle Balls, 176

**K**

Key Lime Pie, 121
Kheer (Indian Rice Pudding), 152
knives, about, 16

**L**

Lemon Love Cupcakes, 106
Lemon Poppyseed Truffles, 175
Linzer Torte, 134

**M**

Macadamia(s): about 5
Macadamia Nut Nut Blondies, White Choco-
    late, 76

Mango-Pistachio Kulfi Pops, 159
Maple Streusel Coffee Cake Squares, 97
maple syrup, about, 10
Marzipan Buckeye Bars, 82
Matt's Banana-Oat Breakfast Bars, 86
Measuring utensils, 16
Midnight Mocha Cookies, 46
Milk(s):
  Coconut, 28
  Oat, 28
  Instant Nut, 26
  Instant Seed, 27
  Nondairy, 25
  Nut, 25
  Seed, 27
mixing bowls and containers, 16

**N**

New York Cheesecake, 104
Nondairy chocolate chips, about, 9
nondairy milks, 25
Not-Your-Grandma's Banana Pudding, 148
Nut Butter, how to make, 34
Nut Milk, 25
nut milk bag, 16
Nut Milk, Instant, 26
nutrition, 2-3
nuts and seeds, about, 4; soaking, 6
Nutty Buddy Sandwiches, 54

**O**

Oat(s): about, 9
  Flour, 9; recipe, 32
  Milk, 28
oils, about, 7
Ooey Gooey Caramel Sauce, 191
Options Guide, 21

**P**

pans, 16
Pantry List, 18

Peach Cobbler, Vanilla Bean, 140
Pecan(s): about, 5
  Chai Spice Bars, 85
  Shortbread Cookies, 60
Pie(s) and Tart(s):
  Blueberry Dream, 124
  Coco-Nana Cream, 127
  Dark Chocolate Truffle Tart with Macaroon
    Crust, 130
  Deep-Dish Caramel Apple, 118
  French Silk, 122
  Individual Cherry Crumbles, 137
  Key Lime, 121
  Linzer Torte, 134
  Strawberries & Crème Tart, 138
  Summer Fruit Pizza, 117, 128
  Tropical Fruit Tartlets, 133
  Vanilla Bean Peach Cobbler, 140
Pineapple Upside-Down Cake, 98
pistachios, about, 5
protein, 2
Protein Crinkle Cookies, 63
protein powder, 14
Protein Power Pudding, 150
Puddings, Ice Creams, and Pops:
  about puddings, 143
  Banana Soft-Serve, 162
  Create-Your-Own Ice Cream, 156
  Dark Chocolate Sorbet, 160
  Dulce de Leche Spooncream, 151
  Easy Chia Pudding, 144
  Gelato di Avocado, 163
  Kheer (Indian Rice Pudding), 152
  Mango-Pistachio Kulfi Pops, 159
  Not-Your-Grandma's Banana, 148
  Protein Power, 150
  Sugar-Free Chocolate Pudding, 154
  Velvety Chocolate Mousse, 147
pumpkin seeds, about, 7

**R**

raisins, as sweeteners, 13

Raspberry Coulis, 192
raw diet, benefits of, 3
Resources, 199
Russian Tea Cakes, 49

## S

Salted Tahini Caramels, 169
sauces: *See* "Topping(s), Frosting(s), and Sauce(s)."
Sea salt, 14
Seed Milk, 27
seeds: *See* "Nuts and Seeds."
Sesame seeds, about, 7
soaking nuts and seeds, 6
Sorbet, Dark Chocolate, 160
Spices, using, 14
Squeeze bottles, 16
Stand mixer, 17
stevia, about, 11
Storebought staples, 15
Strainer/colander, 16
Strawberry(-ies):
  & Crème Tart, 138
  Blondies, 74
  Shortcupcakes, 110
substitutions and variations, about, 20
Sugar Cookie Cutouts, 44
Sugar-Free Chocolate Ganache, 194
Sugar-Free Chocolate Pudding, 154
Summer Fruit Pizza, 128
Sunflour, about, 10; recipe for, 31
Sunflower Seed Butter, about, 8
Sunflower seeds, about, 7
Sunseed Butter, 37
superfoods, about, 15, 181
Superfood Snackers, 180
sweeteners, about, 10-12

## T

tahini, about, 8
Tangy Cream Cheese Icing, 190
tarts: *See* "Pies and Tarts."

tips and tricks, 20
Topping(s), Frosting(s), and Sauce(s):
  Coconut Lemon Curd, 193
  Fat-Free Chocolate Syrup, 195
  Fluffy Chocolate Frosting, 189
  Fruity Chia Jam, 196-197
  Ooey Gooey Caramel Sauce, 191
  Raspberry Coulis, 192
  Sugar-Free Chocolate Ganache, 194
  Tangy Cream Cheese Icing, 190
  Vanilla-Coconut Crème, 188
Tropical Fruit Tartlets, 133
Truffles:
  Classic Cacao, 172
  Lemon Poppyseed, 175
  White Chocolate Vanilla Bean, 174
Turtle Bites, 177
Tuxedo Cheesecake Brownies, 70

## U

Ultimate Raw Brownies, 67
Utensils, 16

## V

Vanilla Bean Peach Cobbler, 140
vanilla beans, 15
Vanilla-Coconut Crème, 188
Velvety Chocolate Mousse, 147

## W

Walnuts, about, 5
White Chocolate Macadamia Nut Blondies, 76
White Chocolate Vanilla Bean Truffles, 174

# Also from Vegan Heritage Press

Vegan Heritage Press is an independent book publishing company dedicated to publishing products that promote healthful living and respect for all life. Our goal is to bring to the marketplace innovative vegan cooking ideas that will delight longtime vegans, inspire newcomers, and intrigue the curious who want to improve their health and the world around them by preparing excellent plant-based recipes.

## Nut Butter Universe
### Easy Vegan Recipes with Out-Of-This-World Flavors
ROBIN ROBERTSON

Just a small amount of nut butter can add great texture, flavor, and nutrition to your meals. This book is filled with recipes using delectable butters made from cashews, Brazil nuts, macadamias, chestnuts, almonds, and more, including everyone's favorite: peanut butter. *Nut Butter Universe* is a culinary treasure, filled with creative ways to make delicious protein-rich recipes for breakfast, lunch, dinner, dessert, and snacks. Paperback, 172 pages, ISBN: 978-0-9800131-7-7, 16 pages color photos, $18.95.

## Practically Raw
### Flexible Raw Recipes Anyone Can Make
AMBER SHEA CRAWLEY

This truly innovative raw food recipe book offers cooked options on many of the recipes. Also new is that all 140 dishes can be made with or without specialized equipment or ingredients. With creative, satisfying recipes, clever tips, and full-color photos, the book will appeal to seasoned raw foodists, newbies, and anyone who wants flexible, high-nutrition food. Paperback, 256 pages, ISBN: 978-0-9800131-5-3, full-color throughout, $19.95.

## Vegan Fire & Spice
### 200 Sultry and Savory Global Recipes
ROBIN ROBERTSON

Take a trip around the world with delicious, mouthwatering recipes ranging from mildly spiced to nearly incendiary. Explore the spicy cuisines of the U.S., South America, Mexico, the Caribbean, Europe, Africa, the Middle East, India, and Asia with Red-Hot White Bean Chili, Jambalaya, Szechuan Noodle Salad, Vindaloo Vegetables, and more. Organized by global region, this book gives you 200 inventive and delicious recipes for easy-to-make international dishes, using readily available ingredients. You can adjust the heat yourself and enjoy these recipes hot — or not. Paperback, 268 pages, ISBN: 978-0-9800131-0-8, $18.95.

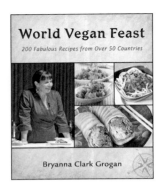

# World Vegan Feast
## 175 Homestyle Recipes from 38 Countries

BRYANNA CLARK GROGAN

Leading vegan cooking expert Bryanna Clark Grogan shares recipes from her 22 years of experience in international cuisines. The book includes authentic dishes from around the world, an international bread sampler, gluten-free and soy-free options, as well as helpful sidebars, tips, and menus. This book features recipes you won't find in other vegan cookbooks. Paperback, 272 pages, ISBN: 978-0-9800131-4-6, 36 color photos, $19.95

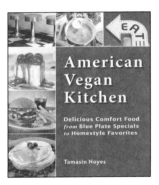

# American Vegan Kitchen
## Delicious Comfort Food from Blue Plate Specials
## to Homestyle Favorites

TAMASIN NOYES

Use these recipes to make your own vegan versions of favorite comfort food dishes found in diners, delis, and cafes across America. They satisfy vegans and non-vegans alike with deli sandwiches, scrumptious burgers and fries, pastas, pizzas, omelets, pancakes, casseroles, and desserts. Paperback, 232 pages, ISBN: 978-0-9800131-1-5, $18.95.

# Vegan Unplugged
## A Pantry Cuisine Cookbook and Survival Guide

JON ROBERTSON WITH RECIPES BY ROBIN ROBERTSON

Vegan Unplugged is your go-to source for gourmet pantry cooking. These easy recipes can be made in fifteen minutes or less. The book is ideal for camping, boating, or anytime you just don't feel like cooking. It's also a "must have" during power outages with great-tasting, nutritionally balanced pantry cuisine. Paperback, 216 pages, ISBN: 978-0-9800131-2-2, $14.95.

# The Blooming Platter Cookbook
## A Harvest of Seasonal Vegan Recipes

BETSY DIJULIO

A celebration of fresh, seasonal produce, this book features a wide range of recipes from easy homestyle dishes to creative upscale fare including American favorites and global cuisines. The 175 recipes showcase the taste, beauty, and nutrition of seasonal ingredients. Also includes recipe variations, menu suggestions, seasonal icons, and tips. Paperback, 224 pages, 36 color photos, ISBN: 978-0-9800131-3-9, $18.95.